"Dorothy L. Sayers' vivid pe
drawing in both those long
work, and those who have ye.. .. ..
Gina Dalfonzo, author of *Dorothy and Jack: The transforming friendship of Dorothy L. Sayers and C.S. Lewis*

"This insightful biography is essential and enjoyable reading for all who are interested in discovering more about the extraordinary life of Dorothy L. Sayers."
Monika B. Hilder, Professor of English, Trinity Western University, and co-editor of *The Inklings and Culture: A harvest of scholarship from the Inklings Institute of Canada*

"For the person who has been captivated by her Lord Peter Wimsey stories or is aware of her connection with C. S. Lewis but does not yet know her, this treatment of Sayers is a must-buy."
Dr Hal L. Poe, Charles Colson Professor of Faith and Culture at Union University in Jackson, Tennessee

"With vivid descriptions that bring Sayers' rich inner life and powerful imagination alive, this biography is an authoritative and commanding addition to the lexicon of Sayers' world."
Patti Callahan, NYT bestselling author of *Becoming Mrs Lewis*

"Colin Duriez has presented us with a portrait of a brilliant and emotionally sensitive woman, whose real-life struggles and achievements are even more compelling reading than her fictional plots."
Fiona Veitch Smith, author of the 'Poppy Denby Investigates' Series

"This is a very vivid and readable introduction to Dorothy L. Sayers' life and work that is both comprehensive and engaging."
Revd Dr Jeanette Sears, Former Tutor in Doctrine and Church History, and author of *Murder and Mr Rochester*

DOROTHY
A BIOGRAPHY
L. SAYERS

*Death, Dante, and
Lord Peter Wimsey*

COLIN DURIEZ

LION

DEATH

Death, be not proud, though some have called thee
Mighty and dreadful, for thou art not so;
For those whom thou think'st thou dost overthrow
Die not, poor Death, nor yet canst thou kill me.
From rest and sleep, which but thy pictures be,
Much pleasure; then from thee much more must flow,
And soonest our best men with thee do go,
Rest of their bones, and soul's delivery.
Thou art slave to fate, chance, kings, and desperate
men,
And dost with poison, war, and sickness dwell,
And poppy or charms can make us sleep as well
And better than thy stroke; why swell'st thou then?
One short sleep past, we wake eternally
And death shall be no more; Death, thou shalt die.

John Donne (1572–1631), from *Holy Sonnets*

Dorothy L. Sayers was familiar with and loved this poet's works
from before her college days.

Published by
Lion Hudson Limited
Prama House, 267 Banbury Road,
Summertown, Oxford OX2 7HT, England
www.lionhudson.com

ISBN 978 0 7459 5692 3
e-ISBN 978 0 7459 5693 0

First edition 2021

Acknowledgments

Extracts pp. 122-23, 142 taken from *C.S. Lewis: Essay collection and other short pieces*, ed. Lesley Walmsley © C.S. Lewis Pte. Ltd 1947. Reprinted by permission.

Extract p. 124 taken from *The Times*. Reproduced by permission.

Extracts pp. 126-27 taken from *Talking About Detective Fiction* by P.D. James, reproduced by permission of Greene & Heaton Ltd.

Extract p. 161 taken from *C.S. Lewis: A companion and guide*, ed. Walter Hooper © C.S. Lewis Pte. Ltd 1947. Reprinted by permission.

Extract p.162 taken from *Miracles* by C.S. Lewis © C.S. Lewis Pte. Ltd 1947. Reprinted by permission.

A catalogue record for this book is available from the British Library

Printed and bound in the United Kingdom, April 2021, LH26

In memory of
John and Evangeline Paterson
Geographer, and Poet

Contents

Preface 10

1. Looking Back: To the Beginning and Later on
   (1893–97, 1943) 15

2. Bluntisham and Salisbury: Schooling at Home and
   Away (1898–1912) 29

3. Somerville College, Oxford (1912–15) 50

4. Poetry, Publishing, and a Try at Teaching (1916–20) . . .70

5. An Accidental Birth and Complex Domesticity
   (1921–26). 89

6. Guinness Was Good for Her (1922–29) 107

7. Lord Peter Wimsey and Eric the Skull: Within the
   Golden Age of the Detection Club (1930–36) 120

8. From Page to Stage: Telling the Greatest Story
   (1936–51). 134

9. A New Love: Rebooting Dante and *The Divine Comedy*
   (1944–57). 153

Epilogue. 176

Dorothy L. Sayers: A chronology. .178

Appendix: Charles Williams' review of *The Nine Tailors*
   by Dorothy L. Sayers 187

Select Bibliography. 189

Notes 195

Index 213

Preface

Dorothy L. Sayers (1893–1957), best known for her detective stories about Lord Peter Wimsey, was in a circle of friends mainly destined to become lifelong friends. They first met together while wartime students at Oxford's Somerville College. In fun, she called the group the "Mutual Admiration Society" (MAS), and the name stuck. Outside of the circle she also was to become a friend of C.S. Lewis and other contemporary writers such as T.S. Eliot and Charles Williams. She contributed to *Essays Presented to Charles Williams*, edited by Lewis as a posthumous tribute from friends. Her series of BBC Radio plays, *The Man Born to Be King*, on the life of Christ, was immensely popular in Britain during the Second World War. In this period, thanks to Charles Williams, she discovered Dante's *The Divine Comedy*, and translated it from medieval Italian into fresh, contemporary English (a task completed after her death by a close friend, Barbara Reynolds).

Though a brilliant scholar, Sayers immediately turned from an academic life after college to a brief period in teaching and publishing, followed by over eight years as an advertising copywriter and "ideas man" (which included the creation of the famous Guinness ads). This provided an income to support her writing. Her success as a crime novelist eventually allowed her to leave advertising and to provide, as an unmarried mother, for her young son. Later, she also supported her journalist husband whose war wounds increasingly affected his quality of life.

As well as a star of the Golden Age of detective fiction, her robust popular theological writings such as *The Mind of the Maker* (1941) revealed a sharp and brilliant mind which, like those of Lewis and G.K. Chesterton, delighted in Christian dogma and orthodoxy. As well as her BBC Radio dramas, she became author of plays for the stage, books on popular theology, on the place of work in understanding our humanity, on female emancipation, as well as on the healing of society and culture after the destruction of war.

Her creative imagination and experience of writing was always in some way part and parcel of her attractive understanding of Christian creeds such as God as Trinity, and the incarnation of Christ, which she presented for modern readers. Relatedly she explored divine and human creativity. Her exuberant faith was captured in both her fiction and non-fiction, written during a life that was far from the quiet confines of academia as it existed at that time. She was one of several important lay theologians who commanded enthusiastic audiences (such as C.S. Lewis, G.K. Chesterton, T.S. Eliot and Charles Williams). She revealed the enormous contribution that lay theology could make to people's lives. She had an emphasis, like Lewis, on "mere Christianity", which is why she stuck to the creeds and Scripture rather than promoting any particular denomination.

C.S. Lewis wrote a heartfelt panegyric to Dorothy L. Sayers, which was read out at the memorial service shortly after her death, concluding, "Let us thank the Author who invented her."

* * * * *

After working for many years on books and articles on C.S. Lewis, J.R.R. Tolkien, and their informal group of friends – the Inklings – I became more and more aware of important affinities between Dorothy L. Sayers and C.S. Lewis, Charles Williams, and even Tolkien – who was bluntly averse to her introducing a love interest into her Lord Peter Wimsey stories. It was not until I started research for this book that I quite suddenly realized how important Sayers' friendships with Lewis and Williams were to her – and also to them.

Having picked up on my interest in Sayers, Ali Hull, at that time a commissioning editor with Lion Hudson, suggested I might write a biography of Sayers, after she had asked what new book I might do for the publisher. Other colleagues of hers were interested, including Tony Collins, who had published my first book on Tolkien many years before for Monarch books. I could not resist Ali's suggestion. Lion Hudson had already published my biographies of Tolkien and of Lewis and had been successful with foreign editions, which were important to me.

Thinking it over, I discovered my interest in Sayers went back a long way. When I gave occasional tours of Oxford to students and others interested in Lewis, Tolkien, and the Inklings, I became increasingly aware of places in the city associated with Sayers – I realized that I had kept mentioning her as I talked of the places frequented by these writers.

Once planted in my mind, I went back to my reading of Sayers and her life, this time more deeply. In my research for this book there are many to whom I am grateful for my better understanding of Dorothy L. Sayers. What was the "L" in her name all about? Why did she hide the existence of her son? My thanks in particular go to the work of Barbara Reynolds, an outstanding scholar and engaging writer, who became Sayers' goddaughter days before Sayers' sudden, unexpected death. I greatly enjoyed Reynolds' affectionate and highly detailed 1993 biography of her godmother. Her in-depth book on Sayers' involvement with the great medieval poet, Dante, adds a rich dimension to the earlier biography. Was the queen of the Golden Age of crime-writing in love with Dante, so much so that she turned from an abundant life of tales about crime, and much of her attachment to Lord Peter Wimsey, to the long but fulfilling years of translating *The Divine Comedy,* one of the greatest poems, and stories, of all time?

As rich were the resources provided by the five volumes edited by Reynolds of thousands of Sayers's letters, with the fifth volume taken up by two unfinished autobiographical pieces covering Sayers' early life, one fictionalized and one direct autobiography, I also found resources in earlier biographies: Janet Hitchman's sometimes overlooked *Such a Strange Lady*, James Brabazon's Dorothy L. Sayers, and Ralph E. Hone's *Dorothy L. Sayers: A Literary Biography*. Many other books followed in a number of countries, mostly focusing on Sayers' thought, social concerns, writings and broadcasts, creativity, and faith, often with biographical touches. Some books came from significant academic dissertations even before a more recent awareness of Sayers' important contribution to scholarship as an independent scholar, though her aim was often toward a wider audience.

My thanks must also go to important places providing resources that I was able and delighted to make use of: the public library in Witham, the then small town where Sayers lived for much of her later life, which has a Dorothy L. Sayers Centre, tastefully crammed with resources; The Wade Center at Wheaton College, Illinois, USA, which has the largest collection on Sayers that I know, and which boasts accessible staff who are expert on all aspects of Sayers; and the famous Bodleian Library in Oxford, the city loved by Sayers. I am grateful to the knowledgeable assistance given me in these places. Among many who helped, I must mention Laura Schmidt and Marj Meade at the Wade, and Seona Ford, Chair of the Dorothy L. Sayers Society (who conveniently lives down the road from the Witham Study Centre, and whose father was a friend of Sayers). My gratitude goes also to the three who helpfully looked at the manuscript in process, willingly giving their perspective on it: Seona Ford, Revd Dr Jeanette Sears, and Dr Gillian Ania.

Finally, I owe my thanks to editors and others at Lion

Hudson who put so much effort into the preparation and production of my book, coping with my anticipated visit to Australia during the busiest time in the schedule, a visit abandoned last minute by travel restrictions caused by the rapid spread of Covid-19. Thanks in particular to Jon Oliver, Joshua Wells, Lyn Roberts, Louise Titley, Miranda Lever, and Katie Carter. I've also appreciated encouragement from friends around the world, often on social media, eagerly awaiting the publication. It is also heartening to see, even now, engaging and delightful books appearing that feature Sayers strongly and importantly, though published too late for me to utilize fully in this book, such as, in order of appearance, Mo Moulton's *Mutual Appreciation Society* (it was great to meet you at your launch in Blackwell's, Oxford, Mo Moulton!), Francesca Wade's *Square Haunting*, and Gina Dalfonzo's *Dorothy and Jack*.

1

Looking Back: To the Beginning and Later On (1893–97, 1943)

I am writing to ask if you would allow me to confer upon you the Degree of D.D. [Doctor of Divinity] in recognition of what I regard as the great value of your work....

William Temple, the Archbishop of Canterbury[1]

The recollections of friends and neighbours, as well as extant letters, can sometimes give quite a vivid impression of single days – and highly significant ones at that – in the life path of Dorothy Leigh Sayers.[2] She was someone you would notice.

Let us go to one day in wartime – Saturday, 4 September 1943, to be precise – when the popular author received a letter which greatly surprised, pleased, and alarmed her in equal measure. Sayers was at home in the small town of Witham, Essex, which is a station on the train line from London to Colchester on the eastern coastal plain of England, and stands on the ancient Roman road between those places. She was there by preference rather than at her apartment in London, where her work tended to be interrupted by visitors. She presumably took breakfast promptly at 8:30 that day as usual, and it was over the meal that she would have opened the formally addressed letter to "Miss Sayers". Her husband, Major Oswald Arthur "Atherton" Fleming, was likely to be just about heard resurrecting in his distant bedroom, or may have gone for his bath also in the part of the house which had once been located next door, before being connected to their house after being bought by Sayers for this purpose.

During her own leisurely after-breakfast bath we can expect her to be turning over the contents of the letter in her ever-active mind, neglecting her habit of reading or working in the comfortable suds. No doubt sometimes her lengthy immersion in the bath gave her some respite from the demands of domestic life, and the storms of her sometimes tetchy husband, long troubled by disorders from the previous war over a quarter of a century ago.

After the bath the domestic chores could resolutely be faced, like the Saturday shopping. This was a task complicated by wartime austerity. A growing list of items were now rationed. Dorothy Sayers would have carried her small, neat ration book as she went from shop to shop along the main street of the compact but bustling town. There were vegetables to get from the greengrocer, meat from the butcher, bread and perhaps cakes from the baker, and, for rare items like cheese, biscuits, jam, and tea, she would, in hope, enter the grocer's shop – the door of which rang a bell when she opened it to alert staff to a customer's arrival.

Sayers, purposely as usual, walked down the street toward the centre of town in her mustard-brown two-piece outfit with its rather long jacket, in beige-coloured stockings and stout brown shoes. Crowned with a black velour hat, the tall, bulky woman could seem formidable. She might have noticed a neighbour's small boy, who perhaps jolted memories of her son

John Anthony, from fifteen years or so ago. Unknown to her, the boy might even have been the one who remembered years later that he thought Mrs Fleming looked a bit like a battleship as she steadfastly surged down the street, avoiding the occasional car as she crossed the road to get to a shop on her list. A charitable boy might have acknowledged in his mind however that she was always pleasant to him, and he may even have observed a characteristic but almost secret smile that made her much less formidable.

That Saturday morning in early autumn, as she proceeded through town, we can expect that she was all the time pondering the letter she had received, and how to respond to it. It began:

> Dear Miss Sayers,
> I am writing to ask if you would allow me to confer upon you the Degree of D.D. [Doctor of Divinity] in recognition of what I regard as the great value of your work especially *The Man Born to Be King* and *The Mind of the Maker*. I have consulted the Regius Professor of Divinity at Oxford who cordially approves my going forward.[3]

It was signed by William Temple, the Archbishop of Canterbury.

It was some days before Sayers hesitatingly replied, asking whether the offer could be changed to that of a D. Litt., a Doctor of Letters, as she felt that she did not deserve a divinity degree. She pointed out that she had come to writing both the series of broadcast plays, *The Man Born to Be King,* and the book, *The Mind of the Maker,* as an established writer rather than a "Christian person". It was essential to her work that she was free to write, even if it meant using the vernacular of the street, should the story require it. While she was clear that the divinity degree was not intended as an emblem of the sacred, she would feel more at her ease if she stood as a notable and acceptable type of Christian. She added that she was never convinced that she truly was one, or had rather perhaps only been enamoured by what had been called "an intellectual pattern", thinking of her friend Charles Williams.

Dorothy Sayers had always been deeply aware that her Christian beliefs were not fundamentally undergirded by deep religious emotion (like John Wesley feeling his heart "strangely warmed" at his conversion), and remarkably, just weeks before, her friend Charles Williams had challenged her over whether her expressed Christian convictions were too much based on its powerful dogmas, which he felt was a harmful position in their day. This was a challenge he had also put to himself. After mentioning how they had recently discussed the intellectual pattern of belief they both loved, Williams had written:

> ...I feel that this matter... is very serious
> indeed. There is a point at which you and
> I will no longer be able to get away with an
> explanation of how admirable we think the
> pattern is, and I think that point is very near
> for both of us. I know as well as you do of the
> bye-ways [sic] of the literary mind, but I do
> not feel that they are going to be much excuse.
> There are awful moments when I think that
> perhaps it is precisely people like us who are
> enthralled by the idea and stop there who
> are really responsible for a great deal of the
> incapacity and the harm [presumably, over
> the effects of the way Christian belief was
> championed at that time].[4]

Sayers characteristically did believe, however, in the truly passionate nature of the intellect, and it was in the white heat of her reasoning power that she wrote her famous mystery stories with their ordered world, and penned her pieces on Christian dogma and on the Christian basis for valuing women as fully human beings with brains rather than as beings limited to tightly predefined roles in society. She also felt very deeply the reality of sin in human lives, and in the corporate guilt thus shared.[5] As well as the danger of being associated too much with the church, weakening her artistic work as a writer, a deeper worry for her in accepting the Lambeth degree would be how this could inspire the popular press to delve into her private life as a celebrity writer. She thought of her closely guarded secret of her son, and how as a single parent she'd had to arrange for a close older cousin to raise him for her. The situation was even more complex because of the child's accidental conception "out of wedlock", as it was expressed in those days; along with the child being labelled "illegitimate" or a "bastard". Then there was the fact that, soon after, she had married a divorced man who was not the father (but who was party to the secret), and any divorce was heavily frowned upon in 1943. She also couldn't ignore the way her BBC Radio plays about the life of Christ, with Jesus representing the straight speech of a real first-century man, had been savaged by many conservative Christians who had not even listened to the broadcasts but nevertheless judged them as blasphemous. She had enjoyed the battle to keep them on air, however.

The writer continued to share her misgivings with the sympathetic archbishop, and eventually declined the honour with his blessing.[6] The shopping, the everyday household chores, and her primary work of writing continued as usual, resolutely driven by her vision of life and her calling as an artist and a maker.

* * * * *

Sayers once said she was "a citizen of no mean city"[7] in an unfinished memoir, quoting from Saint Paul, on Tarsus. The city in her case was Oxford, England, where she was born, spent her early life, later returned to study at Somerville College, and then came back to again in order to work for a publisher for a time. She had relations here for a period – her widowed aunt Maud, and her cousin Margaret Leigh whose undergraduate study at Somerville overlapped with hers. Her son, John Anthony Fleming, would one day study at Balliol, the college of her detective creation Lord Peter Wimsey. She would in later years visit her Oxford friend C.S. Lewis occasionally and, more frequently, Charles Williams in the last years of his life. The city was, without hesitation, her first love. She saw it as different from any other in the world. Going there made her feel she was coming home. In one of Sayers' last mystery novels, *Gaudy Night* (1935), where she vividly creates the fictional Shrewsbury College in Oxford, the female detective Harriet Vane speaks for her author when she similarly endorses the city. It was the living city of her dreams. In another story of the 1930s, Harriet marries Lord Peter Wimsey at Oxford's St Cross Church, where Charles Williams would one day be buried.

Accounts made of Sayers' childhood are inevitably dominated by her memories of it, due to the unfinished memoir and a companion incomplete novel of hers intended in part to capture her childhood.[8] In these, written around the beginning of her forties, she displays an extraordinary recollection of a number of particular events, including many from her first four-and-a-half years, when she started life in Oxford. These early memories capture some of the eccentricities of the city, which more than likely helped to determine the unusual life of the child prodigy.

The only child of Revd Henry Sayers, MA, and Helen Mary "Nell" Sayers, née Leigh, was born within earshot of the famous sound of the great bell of the Tom Tower of Christ Church as summer approached in 1893. Dorothy's first home, 1, Brewer Street, was located at the Christ Church Choir School, down the narrow-cobbled road off St Aldate's in Oxford. The house now carries a blue plaque inscribed:

Dorothy L. Sayers
Writer and Scholar
was born here
13 June 1893

From Brewer Street, just across St Aldate's thoroughfare, lies the large college of Christ Church itself. Dorothy's father was headmaster of the Choir School and a chaplain at Christ Church Cathedral. Henry and Nell had been married the previous year, Nell joining Henry in Oxford from Shirley, near Southampton. Nell's ancestors were mainly unremarkable landed gentry on the Isle of Wight, off the south coast from Southampton. Her father, Frederick Leigh, in contrast, was a distinguished solicitor, Latin scholar, practical Christian, humourist (he occasionally contributed to the satirical periodical, *Punch*), and was active in the Liberal Party. Of the Leigh family, writer Margaret Leigh, a younger cousin of Dorothy, in her memoir, *The Fruit in the Seed*, spoke of Aunt Mabel's obsession with genealogy (something for which Dorothy had a flair): "I had an aunt who asserted that the Isle of Wight Leighs were descended from the royal house of Wessex. Having proved to her own satisfaction that she was the thirty-second cousin of King Alfred, she kept among her treasures a replica of the jewel that lies at the Ashmolean in Oxford."[9] When Dorothy was christened on 15 July in Christ Church Cathedral, Henry, as chaplain, performed the baptism.

A few months afterwards, early in 1894, the family moved along to the more spacious and neighbouring number 3, Brewer Street, a move auguring further changes ahead for the family.

Though born in Norfolk, Henry had distant Irish roots in County Tipperary, and one of his achievements was that of his being a fellow student at Magdalen College, Oxford, with Oscar Wilde. They appear together with others in an informal photograph. Of her parents, though it was Henry who had the Oxford degree, it was from her mother that Dorothy inherited her sparkling intelligence and fluent use of a pen. Henry, at six foot two, did pass on some distinctive genes to his child which would make her tall for a woman, as people often observed. Unusually for the period, her father encouraged Dorothy, whom he adored, to aim for study at Oxford and, with this in mind, would begin teaching her Latin at the age of seven. His engagement with and delight in music was also passed on to his daughter. Sayers acknowledged that he must have been dull company for his mother, who had never been inclined to marry a man of the cloth, and celebrated her mother by acknowledging the Leigh lineage in her insistence upon being known as an author by the name Dorothy L. Sayers, "L." indicating "Leigh". Sayers, however, would have clergymen in her novels that are cast in a positive light, all of whom have recognizable traits of Henry in their characters, particularly the affectionate rendering of Reverend Theodore Venables in her magnificent story, *The Nine Tailors* (1934).

Nell Sayers comes over as being isolated enough without losing her husband at times to the hidden ceremonies of the Freemasons. Sayers suspected that her father had not really taken to teaching, which is why he went for a rural living after nearly six years of marriage. That he did make some effort in his role as headteacher, however, is evident as he later (but in an oddly restrained way) fondly remembered what he could of unrecorded life at the school house in Brewer Street. Recalling them caused some pain for Henry, even though these had been usually pleasant days. This was true even when he felt he could still hear the benign chimes from Tom Tower, uttering the farewell call to turn off the lights.

Henry's reference to the chiming bell from nearby Tom Tower is a reminder of just how eccentric and often surprising Oxford life can seem to an outsider, and how normal to a participant in it. The ringing at 9:05 each evening was used by the Choir School for lights out, which echoes an original purpose of the chimes for centuries as the beginning of the nightly curfew for Oxford's university students: the students had to be within their respective college gates by this time. The eccentricity is deepened by the fact that the bell tolled from 9:05 p.m., rather than from 9:00 p.m., as might be expected. There was a clear reason for this in the eyes of the Oxford scholars. Oxford Mean Time, judged by latitude, is in fact five minutes behind Greenwich[10] Mean Time (GMT, of course, is historically the defining point of planetary-time demarcation). Tom Tower stands in one of the most imposing and magnificent of Oxford's many colleges, and was designed by Sir Christopher Wren in the seventeenth century; the authoritative bell-ringing added to its character, symbolizing the dominance and distinction of the seat of learning.

The eccentricity doesn't end there. The bell-ringing at 9:05 presents another puzzle for those unfamiliar with the arcane world of the famous university. Thomas Hardy portrays the mystery vividly in his last Wessex novel, *Jude the Obscure* (1895), calling Oxford "Christminster". Jude is a self-educated and intellectually gifted stonemason who longs to be a scholar and who is drawn toward the historic city, with its classical learning and medieval architecture. He eventually journeys there, arriving after the working day is over.

It was a windy, whispering, moonless night.
To guide himself he opened under a lamp a
map he had brought. The breeze ruffled and
fluttered it, but he could see enough to decide
on the direction he should take to reach the
heart of the place.

After many turnings he came up to the
first ancient mediaeval pile that he had
encountered. It was a college, as he could see
by the gateway. He entered it, walked round,
and penetrated to dark corners which no
lamplight reached. Close to this college was
another; and a little further on another; and
then he began to be encircled as it were with
the breath and sentiment of the venerable city.
When he passed objects out of harmony with
its general expression he allowed his eyes to
slip over them as if he did not see them.
A bell began clanging, and he listened till a
hundred-and-one strokes had sounded. He
must have made a mistake, he thought: it was
meant for a hundred.

Jude, however, was right about the number of strokes, but wrong about miscounting. The number of chimes had originally been set as a hundred, to remember the number of students attached to the college. However, when another student was added to the set number in 1663, the toll count was increased to 101.

The experiences and memories of a very young child take a time to fall into place. By the time Dorothy reached a point where, if she were awake at 9:00 p.m., the loud and long chiming would have become part of her normal experience, she was puzzled from being taught that clocks did not strike more than twelve times, whereas old Tom seemed to go on forever. But yet another of Oxford's eccentricities was near at hand, which Dorothy would eventually have as part of her childhood experience, even though it was mainly built up from what she was told by her parents, and probably the domestic staff and others in her life like her aunt Mabel Leigh, Grandmother Sayers and another aunt, Gertrude Sayers, who frequently visited. Representing a rich tradition of nonsense writing, which fitted Dorothy's pronounced sense of humour very well, was a retired don who still had rooms in Christ Church after many years of teaching. Five minutes' walk from Dorothy's home lived Revd Charles Dodgson. She was to love and eventually quote from his "Alice" stories and his poems like "Jabberwocky" which her father delighted to read to her and which she loved to hear. Under his pen name, Lewis Carroll, he already had a great and rapidly growing reputation. The Liddell family, whose daughter Alice was central to, and inspired, his most well-known stories, no longer lived in Christ Church, where her father Henry Liddell had been Dean. Alice, in fact, was by now in her forties and mother of three sons, two of whom in a few years were to die in action in the First World War. Sayers sometimes claimed that a family story of Charles Dodgson having once peered at her in her pram in the famous Christ Church quad was mythical, but nevertheless she would continue to tell the story. Her close friend in later years, Barbara Reynolds, remembers Sayers telling her this encounter as if it were fact.

Dorothy, as an alert and intelligent child, had many other real or constructed memories from the four-and-a-half years that she lived at the Choir School in Brewer Street. Walking in Christ Church's large quad, where was the Mercury fountain with its large fat goldfish, or in the expanse of Christ Church meadows, edged by the flowing Isis river[11] and its large elms perfect for games of hide-and-seek, were familiar experiences.

A well-remembered jaunt was taking in the walks beside Magdalen College, including Addison's Walk, which one day would be much frequented by the Magdalen don C.S. Lewis. This gave Dorothy opportunities for feeding the fallow deer. (In later years, C.S. Lewis remembered J.R.R. Tolkien sweeping off his hat and greeting the deer there with, "Hail fallow well met.") Another memory was both bizarre and comic. Oxford's High Street must rank as one of the most beautiful streets in an English city, and to this day has many smaller shops, rather than being dominated by chain stores, as well as displaying the frontages of colleges, the Examination Schools, and the historic University Church of St Mary the Virgin. It was perhaps in the High Street that a dentist's had in its window a model that never failed to intrigue the young Dorothy. With its display of molars, it was mechanically activated to constantly represent the moving human jaw as it slowly and, for Dorothy, "entrancingly" opened and shut.[12]

Near her house were kept horses that pulled the city trams, and Sayers, years later, vividly remembered the din from iron-rimmed cartwheels and horseshoes on cobbled streets. Another memory was much more significant to her – that of learning to read before the age of four. She remembered being carried downstairs to her mother's bedroom each morning without fail to sit beside her on her bed while Dorothy's mother read to her. As Nell read, Dorothy would look at the open book and follow the shape of the words as her mother came to them. In this way she learned to read without being aware of any effort: in fact, she had no idea that she was learning to read; she simply picked up reading. Her intuitive method of recognizing and learning the "general outline" of particular words long before she mastered the alphabet did not lead to any future difficulty in spelling, as might be expected. She did record one amusing consequence, however. It was when she was brought to church at the age of perhaps five or six that she read the title, "A General Confession" before the prayer "Almighty and most merciful father" as "A General Confusion". She remembers thinking it was a stage direction, indicating the rumble generated by the worshippers as they lowered themselves on to their kneelers in the pews. It was some time later that she achieved spelling out the confounding shape letter by letter, putting right the stamped image. There is even a hint of the future playwright in her reminiscence.

It was not only Nell but Henry Sayers too, who read to their daughter from a wide repertoire; as well as the Alice stories, and nonsense verses like "Jabberwocky", her father introduced her to Uncle Remus' tales of Brer Rabbit, and the folk stories recorded by the brothers Grimm.

Dorothy had a great talent for play throughout her childhood and youth, and retained many happy memories of her exploits with her favoured toy animals, which constantly inspired stories, often enacted in dramas. From very young, she tells us, she could also clearly distinguish between fantasy and reality, so in a sense the future fiction-maker was present in her early stages even then. Two toy monkeys in particular, Jacko and Jocko, helped her to create adventures – she was never at a loss in amusing herself. A pair of scissors removed most of the older monkey's hair, leaving Jacko rather bald, but his failing glass eyes were able to be replaced by brown buttons. Despite Jacko's repulsive appearance, Sayers tells us he was very dear to her. Another toy entered the adventures: a rag doll who, for a reason she couldn't remember, was dubbed "The Frenchman". Perhaps he can be seen as another element of her future in her infancy – a love for French language and literature – to add to her imaginative invention, theatricality, storytelling, and verbal brilliance. Sayers says that he was essential as the villain in all her games, at the receiving end of bumps and thumps.

As the end of 1897 approached, the four-year-old began to sense that a "great change" was on its way, with conversations between the adults in the household about "the new house" and life in "the country" and mysterious goings on, such as her mother and father suddenly becoming greatly interested in a vast book crammed with wallpaper patterns.

2

BLUNTISHAM AND SALISBURY: SCHOOLING AT HOME AND AWAY (1898–1912)

All the world's a stage,
And all the men and women merely players....
William Shakespeare, *As You Like It*[1]

One January day in 1898, after a train journey from Oxford of about eighty miles, four-year-old Dorothy walked from a rural railway station to a nearby grand ivy-clothed house that was set in an expanse of garden, and which was to be her new home. She remembered years later that on this day she had been accompanied by her nurse, Grandmother Sayers, and Aunt Mab (as Aunt Mabel was sometimes called), her toy monkey Jacko, and the family parrot, carried in a cage by her aunt. The station was marked as Bluntisham, and the grand Georgian house was off the Ely road and reached by a winding drive. The rectory (for that is what the house was) stood apparently three storeys high, with its false facia built over the house front to disguise the fact that the building only had two storeys. It was beside St Mary's Church and, like the church, overlooked Bury Fen.[2] Revd Henry Sayers was starting new employment as rector, serving the villages of Bluntisham and close-by Earith. At the rectory,

Dorothy was reunited with her parents and domestic staff – the manservant, the cook, and three maids – all of whom had gone on ahead to Bluntisham a day or two before. The parrot was an important family member, and would play its part in one of Sayers' children's books many years later, as well as frequently and imperiously squawking "Cook" in her Aunt Mabel's voice.

A History of the County of Huntingdon describes the rectory as:

> ...a large two-storied building with a square
> front, built of white brick, concealed by which
> are old attic gables. Its present form dates
> from 1848. In the middle of the front is an old
> doorway, now used as a window, which was
> brought from Cromwell's house in St. Ives,
> when it was pulled down in 1848. The Rectory
> stands in a garden of 3 acres.... The setting
> of the rectory among groups of fine trees and
> flower beds affords an attractive view to those
> who pass along the Ely road.[3]

The living of Bluntisham-cum-Earith, administered by Christ Church, Oxford, had become vacant at a serendipitous time for Henry, who was ready for a new venture and whose voice was giving out.[4] Perhaps the appeal of combining the life of a country gentleman in Huntingdonshire (the living was well paid) with wide-ranging parish duties was focused by the heavy and unrelenting demands of running the Choir School and serving as chaplain to the cathedral. Henry was not a man about town so rural life had no fears for him, as it did for Nell – and besides, the rectory was far more spacious for the family. He would have an expansive study, Nell her own bedroom and sitting room, Dorothy two nurseries – one for the day and one for the night – and there was plenty of space for the domestic staff, as well as for Grandmother Sayers and Aunt Mabel Leigh, to become residents. Dorothy certainly soon felt settled in the area. Forty years later she wrote in a newspaper article that, from the ages of five to thirty-five, the Fen country was her real home.[5]

Now the move was over, any social life had to be created within the large household itself, as Bluntisham was made up mainly of farmers and others employed on the surrounding farms, for which fruit and vegetable growing was predominant at that time. Though the conservative ethos of the area then remained feudal, there was no local squire, and no doctor who lived nearby to provide suitable company for the Sayers. As rector, Henry had multiple functions as he conscientiously served his parish, enjoying his social status among his flock. Nell did not permanently dwell on the disheartening changes in her life, including loneliness, in moving from lively city to unchanging Ruritania, instead pouring her energy to exhaustion into the community. Dorothy's cousin, Margaret Leigh, would spend part of the summer holidays each year staying at the Bluntisham rectory. Younger than Dorothy by a year, she, like Dorothy, was a talented writer, and future author of a number of books. Her memoir, *The Fruit in the Seed,* has a number of vivid impressions of her cousin's family, as well as later life at college in Oxford. Though not particularly impressed by her Uncle Harry (Henry Sayers), Margaret very much took to Dorothy's vivacious mother, pointing out that her

> …aunt was forced into a life she would never
> have chosen for herself. Worldly, quick-witted,
> and sceptical, she hated the Establishment,
> and did not scruple to say so…. She was
> very popular with the poor, especially the old
> women, whom she visited frequently; but had

no use for the farmers' wives, who... wore
hats that made the church pews look like
stalls at a country flower show. Teetotallers
were an abomination to her, and she took a
malicious pleasure in watching them at choir
treats, lapping up the trifle she had plentifully
doped with brandy.... She was a great reader,
even of serious literature, and an admirer of
A.E. Housman and Thomas Hardy, whose
pessimism she shared.[6]

Margaret did not totally disparage her uncle, however, feeling
the need in one place to casually correct her judgment about
him: "My Uncle Harry was a lazy, or should I say leisurely,
parson of the old-fashioned Broad Church type, who, apart
from two services on Sunday and a little parish visiting, lived
the life of a country gentleman."[7] She was unequivocal with
her feelings, however, when she noted: "My uncle, like many
another stupid man with a wife intellectually above him, tried
to assert himself by petty tyranny. In later years, when they had
a car and a wireless set, he never allowed my aunt to touch
either, though she had taught herself to take a clock to pieces,
clean it, and put it together again."[8]

   Dorothy was to fall in love with the often bleak Fen
country of East Anglia, and got to know its distinctive lowland
landscape thoroughly, later placing her novel *The Nine Tailors*
in it, often, but not always, in fictionalized form. Bluntisham
and Earith, Dorothy's home and neighbouring village, lie
within the edges of the large Fen country, a region shaped
by the movement of ice and water during the most recent Ice
Age, with much of the land reclaimed from the risen sea levels
rather as in the Netherlands. The name "Earith" means mud
or gravel; combined with *hithe*, a landing place or small port

("Earth" + "hithe"): before major drainage of the Fen country, the nearby hill area of Ely was an island. The Romans, and perhaps others before them, made great efforts at drainage of the fenland, which were not maintained in later centuries. In the seventeenth century, however, Cornelius Vermuyden and other Dutch engineers were employed to rework the landscape with dykes, vast drainage channels, and sluices, some of the finance coming from the Duke of Bedford. The contrasts of native soil have distinctly shaped the contours of the area, with large areas of peat causing land to sink well below the level of silt expanses as it dried out after drainage.[9] In *The Nine Tailors,* Lord Peter Wimsey tells his butler Melvyn Bunter about the draining of a region (which in fact is in Dorothy's neighbourhood, as well as elsewhere, where the fictional detective was brought up).

Lord Peter refers to Denver Sluice, as well as Earith and other places, in a mainly factual way. That sluice is a feature belonging to an actual village of Denver close to Downham Market. Sayers set her famous creation as having an ancestral home near the village, where Lord Peter's mother lived as Dowager Duchess of Denver. Having the aristocratic detective in her stories as a native of the Fen country is tribute to Sayers' affection for the region.

The versatile writer also was to draw upon her early memories of the Fen country in a magazine article in *The Spectator.* At one point she specifically refers to her childhood there. Sayers recalls that she became used to the constant winter floods. She remembered that, every year, there would always be someone who commented during breakfast that, with the heavy rain they'd been having, the water would be let out through the sluices. Each time, the view from the front windows showed the upper River Ouse overflowing, filling fields with water.[10]

A great flood is an unforgettable sequence in the plot of *The Nine Tailors,* which Sayers based on a deluge of apocalyptical proportions in 1713,[11] and reads for some like a prophecy in that other major floods struck the area some years after the novel's 1934 publication, in 1947 and 1953. Her cousin Margaret Leigh was also taken with the region in her summer holiday stays at the rectory in Bluntisham. The Fen country, she remembered, "was a level land of rich black soil, with wide horizons on which trees and church spires were seen hull down like ships at sea".[12]

From very young, Dorothy had a rich inner life, with her powerful imagination and early talent for self-dramatization. At the same time, her awareness of her Fen country environment often called her out of doors to play in the large rectory garden and to appreciate visiting the next village and other nearby places. She would walk, go for horse-drawn drives, and later, bicycle to nearby places like Earith and St Ives. Her mother appears to have gone off to visit Oxford at least once a year, where still lived her sister Maud, married to a frail Oxford don, with their daughter Margaret. In one letter to her mother in Oxford the young child asks her if she has visited Old Tom at Christ Church. Presumably Nell had told her she would do this. For the fledgling Dorothy, it would have been a sufficient and sensible reason for visiting Oxford. The five-year-old wrote to her mother that she had gone to Earith that afternoon, running all the way with her hoop, and that a farmer's wife her mother was acquainted with had given her an orange (from her fruit-growing). She was also about to have a violin lesson with her daddy. Sayers asked in the letter to give her "best love" to her cousin Margaret, which indicates that Nell was staying with her highly educated sister (one of the first students at Somerville College) in cobbled Holywell, in an old house. Later, after she was widowed in 1904, Maud, together with Margaret, lived in the west of Oxford in Frenchay Road, where from high in the house the sun could be seen sinking behind the nearby Cotswold foothills.

Another letter to her mother who was on a visit to Oxford nearly a year later is more accomplished. Dorothy tells Nell that her daddy had made a snowman for her earlier and that then heavy snowfall had ruined the skating – a common activity in the area.[13] Local people delighted in bandy, a form of ice-skating, which had a celebrated team called Bury Fen Club. The fact that the rectory overlooked Bury Fen, with its winter expanse of frozen water, helped to make skating familiar to the child. Dorothy also confessed in her letter to having thrown snowballs at the dogs. She signed off with her love and "Dossie". This name had caught on for a while in the household after she first attempted to say her name, and it came out as that. In a letter the next month Dorothy proudly proclaimed that she had read out aloud the newspaper's "leading article" about the Boer War to her grandmother and Aunt "Mab". The article may have reported on the Relief of Ladysmith in South Africa at that time.

Henry Sayers surprised Dorothy one morning by coming into her nursery with a Latin primer, intent upon beginning lessons. She was not yet seven. He saw her already as a future student at Oxford, with its challenging entrance requirements. He could little have predicted the enormous role that languages would play in his daughter's life. In his hand, Dorothy remembered, he carried a well-worn black book, and he announced that he thought her now of age to begin learning Latin. The weathered book was by the well-known Victorian writer, Dr William Smith, author of dictionaries, but in this case a guide to Latin, titled *Principia Latina: A First Latin Course*. It was likely that it was then, showing her the declension of *mensa*, that her father pointed out that the Romans were very un-English in changing the ends of their nouns according to the case. Dorothy recalled that she did not find this at all strange, as she found life full of unusual things, such as a beetle having six legs, a spider eight, and a cat only four, and was of course familiar with a bell that tolled many more than twelve times at five minutes after nine o'clock in the evening. Dorothy's young mind was receptive to the wonder of things, while being powerfully logical.

Perhaps at some point Nell, or Dorothy's Aunt Maud, or maybe her genealogy-loving Aunt Mab, told her of her late Great Uncle Percival Leigh. This medically trained amateur actor, friend of Thackeray and Dickens, and humourist contributor to *Punch* magazine, wrote in a single night, it was claimed, the *Comic Latin Grammar: A New and Facetious Introduction to the Latin Tongue* (1840), to raise funds to free an artist friend from a debtor's prison. Interestingly, its nonsense-loving Preface concludes with a note on a new phenomenon of women entering more and more into the world of learning. "The march of intellect is not confined to the male sex; the fairer part of the creation are now augmenting by their numbers, and adorning by their countenance, the scientific and literary train. But the path of learning is sometimes too rugged for their tender feet."[14] To ease this impediment Percival Leigh offers his book as a humble Kidderminster carpet underfoot, he not being poetic enough, he writes, to strew the path of his female readers with roses, "that thus smoothly and pleasantly they may make their safe assent to the temple of Minerva and the Muses."[15] Certainly, for his descendant Dorothy, the learning of Latin was essential for her future path of learning, though she had tough feet and Smith's no-nonsense *Principia* rather than her mischievous great uncle's *Comic Latin Grammar* at her fingertips.

Dorothy would be home-educated for most of her childhood – by her father and mother, and various governesses, whose lessons included German and French. She became fluent in French and developed an equally deep knowledge of German. Later in life she was to describe her youthful education in a now-famous essay entitled "The Lost Tools of Learning", which has been taken up strongly by many of the advocates for the large home-schooling trend in the US; this is despite Sayers' thoughts differing from the famous shaper of home-schooling, pioneer educationalist Charlotte Mason, who was associated with her distinctive teacher training at Ambleside, in the English Lake District.

In "The Lost Tools of Learning" Sayers set out the phases of her own educational development as a child, as she remembered them, and how these phases happily suit the foundational classic stages of medieval learning (the three-fold Trivium[16]). She dubbed the phases of her own experience as the Poll-parrot, the Pert, and then the Poetic. In the Poll-parrot stage she relished rote learning and memorization; in the Pert stage she delighted in challenging and "answering back" (especially to her elders); and in the Poetic phase she said she would by necessity be "difficult". In the Poetic stage, she acknowledged that she was self-centred and eager to express herself. She was restless, and accomplished in making herself to be misunderstood. The aim was success in being independent, and showing an emergent creativity, eagerly working to bring together what she was gaining in knowledge and overall preference.[17]

For Sayers, therefore, looking back on her childhood, the layout of the medieval Trivium adapts beautifully to the three stages she experienced: Grammar (the Poll-parrot), Logic (the Pert), and Rhetoric (the Poetic). The primary pattern of the Trivium, she was certain, provides the tools of learning, which can fluidly adapt to the rich variety of newly encountered knowledge.

These thoughts of her own childhood and education are all to do with her gradual discovery of how human knowledge is interconnected.

Sayers's unfinished memoir, *My Edwardian Childhood* and incomplete *Cat o' Mary*, written in the early 1930s, sets out an unfolding epiphany she experienced of the wonder of joined-up rather than fragmented knowledge. This was to become the foundation of her intellectual development as avid learner and eventually renowned scholar. The epiphany involved several linked experiences, which marked the beginning of a lifetime of putting knowledge together coherently. This made her able to move from being a leading writer in the Golden Age of detective fiction (while working full-time and with great success in a large advertising company), to a playwright actively involved in productions of her work on radio and on stage, to a renowned and bestselling translator of Dante's *The Divine Comedy* from medieval Italian. Behind all this was someone who turned out to be a popular theologian and Christian apologist, along with C.S. Lewis, Charles Williams, G.K. Chesterton, and others. She would write numerous essays on Christian teaching and in defence of it, and a seminal book of theology, *The Mind of the Maker*, where her advanced thinking about the divine Trinity leads to an innovative insight into the very essence of human creativity (featured below in chapter 8). Her essays and books would speak to important topics of her day, including nagging issues raised by the dark years of the Second World War.

* * * * *

What we know of Dorothy's epiphany is laid out in *My Edwardian Childhood* and *Cat o' Mary*. These uncompleted writings operate like a Rosetta Stone when read side by side, in that the memoir deciphers the fictional people and places which are often closely based upon fact. The two writings give another dimension to each other.

A key experience in her epiphany of the unity of knowledge – which was to lay behind her adult writings, work, and thought – was her discovery that history, geography, and literature did not differ, but in fact were one thing.[18] Most of her biblical and theological knowledge was being gained as she sat, stood, and kneeled in the rectory pew at church, where she was immersed in the calendar of Bible readings, the Book of Common Prayer, hymns (often more ancient than modern), and the creeds. Her clerical father appears to have given her no personal religious instruction, but relied upon the experience of church teaching and morning family prayers (also attended by the domestic staff). With her boundless curiosity, Dorothy had become familiar with a wealth of biblical characters, one of which was Ahasuerus from the book of Esther. She then discovered one day, through her lessons and reading in the classics, that Ahasuerus was also known as the king of Persia, Xerxes. She had already discovered that Cyrus the Persian of classical times also appears in the biblical book of Daniel. With these two areas (the Bible and classical history) being recognized by her as related, she began to notice connections everywhere in knowledge. Sayers would in time become adept at synthesizing knowledge, which she delighted to share in her writings – as when the complex art of bell-ringing is woven into the plot of her mystery, *The Nine Tailors*.

Another milestone in her epiphany connected the abstractions of geometry with a very practical problem that Dorothy's father had brought upon himself by errors made laying out a tennis court in the rectory garden. It was located on a lawn that lay in the shade of trees and rarely dried out after rain. One spring had been very wet, and the grass on the lawn grew even more quickly than usual. Henry Sayers wished to insert net-posts so that the court was made ready for tennis. Due to the length of the grass, however, the rector was unable to locate the two iron sockets for the net-posts, or the corner sockets. Flushed by the heat, he accidentally came across one of the net sockets. Nell, in turn, uncovered the measurements of the court in a drawer. Dorothy looked on at the drama. Henry proceeded in a straight line in what he took to be the right direction to a corner, prodding the ground as he went for the iron socket. At this point, Dorothy's schoolwork on Euclidean geometry popped into her mind. She walked to where her father was and told him he was wrong to go in a straight line. Confidently she told him he needed to go in a circle, proceeding to briefly tell her audience of the Euclidean method, based on the properties of the radius of a circle. As she saw the problem's solution in her mind's eye, she remembered, she directly encountered beauty. Sayers was never to find mathematics easy, but here beauty had shown itself again, in the fulfilling oneness of things, as she saw it. It was the marriage of what was learnt with the thing that was accomplished, she reasoned, glimpsing this as the vital accomplishment of the intellect.[19] Measuring a piece of string using the information her mother had found, and tying the string to the net-socket, she pulled it taut and walked in an arc, prodding the ground, and very quickly finding the desired corner socket. In the meantime, by trial and error, Nell had found the next net-socket and, before long, all sockets were located. Dorothy was awestruck. As she put it, she had seen the intersections of the circles stride out alive from the text of her schoolbook on Euclid and meet on her sunlit lawn.[20]

Though she was for a long time inclined to unify reality by intellect, that childhood epiphany was to work out gradually in a wider synthesis that included both poetic imagination and abstract thought. It took exceptional power and creativity on Sayers' part to conceive such a unity of knowledge – or, more properly, to discover it by thought, imagination, and experience together, and embody it in her work.

Another unifying influence on her life from her childhood was her dramatizing, and her ear and eye for drama. Though there was already vision behind it, and imagination, dramatizing had yet to be a highly important part of Dorothy's experience of objective knowledge: knowledge emotional and actual as well as intellectual; knowledge through the body as well as the spirit. She was aware that she was prone to self-dramatization. Through all the fantasies, however, she was clear that she was the creator, and not the lead person – though she often chose to be the hero (more rarely the heroine) of the invented situations. She found herself unable to ignore a dramatic touch.

Her dramatizing can be seen throughout her life, from dressing at home in male costume as her hero Athos for plays and games about the three Musketeers; to flamboyant dress, including spectacular earrings, as an undergraduate; to clowning in meetings of the Detection Club as one of the royals of the Golden Age of mystery stories; and later in life sometimes dressing in three-piece suits in a society dominated by the male. An aspect of this dramatizing that is striking is a gift for dialogue, which indicates her carefully listening to and absorbing conversations at all levels. No matter how close to or distant from the actual ones heard, they display an ear for dialogue that comes out in her stories and plays. In *My Edwardian Childhood* and *Cat o' Mary*, she assuredly recreates conversations. Much of her Golden Age storytelling relies heavily on the momentum of dialogue, which later of course is at the centre of her creative work as a playwright for stage and broadcast.

* * * * *

When Dorothy was in her early teens, and she was deep into her discovery of Alexandre Dumas' *The Three Musketeers*, she called the rectory "Château de Bragelonne" in association with the story, and she was persuading family, domestic staff, friends, and anyone else at hand, to dress or at least play-act in some way as musketeers and characters of the period of Louis XIII, while she swashbuckled as her favourite character, Athos. She considered her father to be Louis XIII and her mother Cardinal Richelieu. When Grandmother Sayers died, some white stockings were urgently needed for the corpse laying at home. Nell asked her daughter if there were any white stockings in her dressing-up clothes. Dorothy was able to hand over stockings she had bought at nearby St Ives for her costume as Athos. As Sayers noted in *Cat o' Mary*, her grandmother was carried to her open grave, adorned with musketeers' stockings.

* * * * *

Soon after Dorothy's immersion in seventeenth-century French life, the rectory received a visit from her cousin, Ivy Shrimpton, daughter of her Aunt Amy of the Leigh side of her family. Ivy was eight years older than Dorothy, and had grown up on a farm in California. When her family returned to England, Ivy studied at a convent school in Oxford, run by Anglican nuns. Ivy became a frequent visitor to Bluntisham. Dorothy had reached the age of worship, and her quickly developing friendship with Ivy gave the single child someone to look up to and admire. Ivy was drawn into the world of musketeers as Marie, Duchess de Chevreuse, who was Athos' lover in the story. Dorothy was already a keen writer of letters, some of them characteristically very long, and a correspondence consistently flowed between the two of them when Ivy returned to her home in Oxford. From the letters, she gives a hint of having somewhat of a rather playful crush on Ivy, and perhaps Dorothy's burgeoning sexuality was making its presence felt. In one very theatrical letter, Dorothy addresses her cousin as if Ivy were Marie and she Athos. That long letter is remarkably consistent, however, in keeping to the voice of Athos amidst its humorously exaggerated sentiment; the letter includes a *rondeau* for Athos' lover that is very accomplished for a fifteen-year-old. The letter acts out a feature of their friendship, the mutual immersion in Dumas' world, and in Dorothy's natural sense of play. Perhaps Ivy's more relaxed Californian upbringing helped to draw her to her younger and exuberant cousin. Ivy's maturity was undoubtedly a steadying influence on her, and, as Sayers remarked about her girlhood in Oxford and Bluntisham, from very young she was able to distinguish fantasy and reality.

The letter can be balanced by others. One recounts to Ivy Dorothy's attraction to a boy of her age whom she and Ivy dubbed "Dull Red", based on the colour of a ball he used when playing on the croquet lawn at the rectory. The boy, Arthur Hutchinson, had visited Bluntisham over the summer of 1907 with his parents, who kept company with the Sayers. Dorothy tells Ivy of her success in being with Dull Red alone over some of the last days he spent in the village, before returning home with his parents. She said that she was now afflicted with an infatuation with him. Another letter, over a year later, informed Ivy that she had fallen helplessly in love. She feared that it was bound to be an unrequited passion, as the person was a well-known actor called Lewis Waller, who was a married man in his late forties. (Dorothy had many rivals, as there existed a "Keen on Waller Club".) She had just seen him in a December performance of Shakespeare's *Henry V* in London, with her parents.

Neither of the cousins dreamed for a moment that their friendship was to prove one of the most important supports in Sayers' momentous life. It was however foreshadowed in a remarkable, and what would turn out to be an almost shockingly prescient, long letter fourteen-year-old Dorothy had written to Ivy in February 1908. After talking about a difficult piece she was attempting to write, and a pleasant concert in which she played the fiddle, she gives Ivy some unrequested advice about how to talk to a cousin she had mentioned, called Freda, presumably in a letter, and then warns her of falling into being a Pharisee. Dorothy feels that Ivy should make more allowances than she does for the mistakes people make. Here Dorothy is preparing the way for an uncertainty she has over her dear cousin. Dorothy then tells Ivy that she wouldn't want to fear to come to her cousin for help if, for instance, she had fallen into a very great sin. This fear would only go if Ivy would try to make allowances for her.

Astonishingly, after the passage of sixteen years, Sayers does approach her friend and cousin over a life-changing event for which she is desperate for help. That event occurs nearly halfway through her life, and dramatically shapes the remainder of it. [21]

Dorothy shared many intimate things with Ivy in her letters, including poems. Ivy was undoubtedly important to the budding writer. Poetry writing, as well as her play scripts, had been a central part of Dorothy's life for quite some time. It had become a habit to share some of them in her correspondence with Ivy, or when Ivy was visiting. As the years of her youth unfolded, her confidence and accomplishment in her poetry writing increased. Having Ivy as reader or audience was an important encouragement to the ever-creative youngster.

* * * * *

When Dorothy was in her fifteenth year, her parents began to plan for her to enter a school. They could do no more for her educationally, and knew that she needed to be prepared for the Oxford University entrance requirements in a couple of years. The best college to aim for, they decided, was that attended by her Aunt Maud – Somerville. As for the necessary two years of senior schooling, there were no accessible day schools in and around the Fen country. Boarding in a distant girls' school would be the best option. After carefully surveying possible places, they decided upon Godolphin School in Salisbury, and began to make preparations. The ideal time for Dorothy to begin there would have been the autumn term of 1908. Her only experience of schooling had been at home, and though some local children had shared her classes, and occasionally children would board at the rectory for this schooling, there was no permanence in their length of attendance, and the numbers were small. With a school like Godolphin, the number of girls was fewer than 200, and most had developed friendships among their class mates. The autumn term would at least be something of a fresh start for everyone after the summer holidays. However, Henry and Nell decided that she should begin in the spring term of 1909 (where, clearly they did not realize, Dorothy was bound to feel an acute sense of being an outsider, even given her own social confidence, and even though they had chosen a small school). Without any school experience, Dorothy had no idea what she was in for. Her only knowledge would have been from reading a fashionable children's school adventure story like *Tom Brown's Schooldays*, or perhaps recent stories of Greyfriars School by Frank Richards. What she did immediately know was that the pattern of her life, so centred on the performing of her plays, and acting out adventures of the musketeers on a grand scale, must change.

Godolphin School was founded under 200 years earlier, in 1726, for eight orphaned young girls of privileged stock, expanding later in the century, and had just recently had a new surge of life, when, in 1890, Miss Mary Douglas became headmistress. At its long-ago founding, the girls were instructed to "dance, work, read, write, cast accounts and the business of housewifery"[22], which was advanced even for the daughters of gentlewomen of the early eighteenth century. In Dorothy's time, the independent school had a wide contemporary curriculum, and was still nestled in its Anglican (Episcopalian) ethos. When there, even though she had been nurtured in a climate of Christian belief, the school aroused her dislike of heightened religiosity and of sentiment over thought (it was "broad church" rather than the "high church" that Dorothy gradually came to favour). This may be reflected in her first mystery novel, written more than a decade later. In it, Lord Peter Wimsey, searching for the office of a Salisbury solicitor as he follows up a lead in a murder enquiry, lunches inadequately near Millford Hill (the location of Godolphin School, then on the outskirts of the city). During the cheerless meal, Wimsey reflects on the historic Cathedral Close, the largest such close in Britain, where he dines. Just like in other cathedral cities, he decides, the mood of the close penetrates every part of Salisbury. Even the food carries a mild taste of books of worship.[23]

Dorothy's arrival with her parents at Godolphin School was in an open fly pulled by an elderly horse. It turned out that her later start in the school year was to be made all the more difficult because of a mistake by Miss Douglas, the headmistress. She had wrongly assumed that the Sayers' daughter was a term past the normal school starting age, and was greatly surprised to meet a tall, slim young women who was clearly not eight years of age. Dorothy was placed in the lower fifth form but was eventually moved into the upper fifth halfway through the term when her abilities began to come out so markedly that they could not be ignored any more, as in her language lessons.

In the confusion of adapting to the patterns and rules of corporate school life, Dorothy took heart at the presence of French on her timetable, and looked forward to her first lesson. When a young teacher appeared in the classroom, she announced in well-spoken French that they would talk about Molière that day. Then she asked if anyone would like to start, and looked around the class hopefully for a raised hand. After she urged several girls without success, the new pupil, Dorothy, raised her arm. The teacher acknowledged her and asked if she would like to say something on the subject. She then put forward several questions, such as, "What did Molière write?", which Dorothy answered fluently and knowledgeably. She couldn't long enjoy the impression she had made, however, as she was immediately and totally bored with being in a class so far behind her in the language.

Dorothy was soon active in all aspects of school life, which included putting her efforts into the wide variety of subjects on the curriculum. There were piano and violin lessons with a strict but imaginative German teacher who became a favourite for Dorothy, and who soon felt that she could ask her pupil if she would be willing to learn to play the viola, as she needed another player for a concert she was setting up to perform in Salisbury. Dorothy was also asked by the school to sing a solo for an end-of-term concert. Dorothy wrote, produced, and acted in school plays with her usual zest, as well as writing frequently for the school magazine. She threw herself into dancing on Saturday nights in the school hall. She wrote home that she had danced with her form teacher, Miss White, to whom she was drawn in her own theatrical way. Dorothy had observed schoolgirl crushes for her to try out as a familiar phenomenon in the only school life she had experienced. Miss White and the German teacher, Fräulein Fehmer, were among her very favourite teachers. There were also school outings, such as to Salisbury's County Hall to hear the Antarctic explorer Sir Ernest Shackleton lecture. Impressed, the constant letter-writer sent him a sonnet she wrote about him, and the great man replied to her. Characteristically, Dorothy copied out his reply in one of her frequent letters to her parents. In all these activities and pursuits, she also fitted in her hobby of photography, for which she eventually won a school prize.

We have two generally differing views of Dorothy's school life: one from her carefully crafted correspondence with her parents, and the other in her unfinished autobiographical novel, *Cat o' Mary*, where the protagonist, Katherine Lammas, closely represents Dorothy in the main.[24] One pole conveys Dorothy's school life as positive and fulfilling; this is in her letters. At the other pole is *Cat o' Mary*, which portrays Katherine's school life as proving to be for her some physical and emotional turmoil. The result is that we can only conclude, in reading both, that Dorothy's school life was both very difficult for her and enjoyable, reflecting her strong personality.

A poem that she was to write while at university may well have been inspired by an event that cut short Dorothy's studies at Godolphin School: there was a major measles outbreak among pupils, of which she was a victim, and nearly died. Afterwards she convalesced in a nursing home. Worried about further illnesses at the school (there was a scarlet fever scare), and Dorothy's state of weakness, her parents decided that she should be at Bluntisham and not at school, doing her preparations for Oxford entrance at home.[25] Her poem is called, "Hymn in Contemplation of Sudden Death". In it the fledgling poet thanks the Lord for her friends, for the love she gave, for the power given her to see with humour and laughter, for the joy that came from good work done, and much more. As she contemplates sudden death, she concludes that there had been no dearth of joy. In fact, the theme of death, and Dorothy's constant sense of comedy, was to flow through the life that had not been snatched away by illness.

Though her feelings about her time at school were mixed, there was much of joy and laughter to which she could look back. The school had acknowledged Dorothy's giftedness when the results came through of her School Certificate exams[26] (essential for university entrance), particularly in French and

German. She had already gained distinctions in 1909 and 1910. At the start of the spring term of 1911, Miss Douglas told the school that Dorothy had come highest out of all England in the Cambridge Higher Local Examination, with distinction in spoken German and French. More important than these outstanding results was the rapturous impact on Dorothy's life of her studies of French and German.

3

SOMERVILLE COLLEGE, OXFORD (1912–15)

Of those Somerville students in the years
immediately preceding the First War, Dorothy L.
Sayers made the most lasting impression both on
her contemporaries and on the outside world.

Vera Brittain, *The Women at Oxford*[1]

The deep shades among the lights of Dorothy's studies at
Godolphin School, and the concentrated tutoring by post of
Miss Mildred White, the French mistress, had been worthwhile.
Dorothy had learned something of the fundamentals of study,
and she was rewarded by winning a Gilchrist Scholarship in
Modern Languages to Somerville College. Her success was
celebrated on a plaque in the school hall. Of her inspiring
teachers, she was to keep in touch with Miss White and with
Fräulein Fehmer, her music mistress. Despite the difficulties in
communication with Germany in time of war, Dorothy was, in
later years, to persist in corresponding with Fräulein Fehmer
until her death in Frankfurt in 1948: she would survive the
allied bombing of her city.

Sayers arrived at Somerville College, off Oxford's Woodstock
Road, to begin her first term on 11 October 1912, a Friday. The

possessions she brought with her included a colourful selection of clothes, as well as many books. The near-deadly measles that had afflicted her at Godolphin School had damaged her head of hair, with some permanent effects, so her chosen attire was intended to compensate for this, such as bright scarfs and dramatic hats and show-stealing earrings. Any illness or stress could at any time threaten significant though temporary hair loss.

A student called Vera Farnell in the year above Sayers, who, like most students, knew nothing of this ailment, recalled the latter's dramatic entrance to breakfast one morning before an early lecture, "wearing a three-inch-wide scarlet riband round her head and in her ears a really remarkable pair of ear-rings: a scarlet and green parrot in a gilt cage pendant almost to each shoulder and visible right across the hall".[2]

Vera Brittain, who started at Somerville two years after Sayers, noted her startling impact on Somerville life in her *The Women at Oxford*. She said Sayers was:

> A bouncing, affable, exuberant young woman,
> she had a vivid and somewhat crude taste in
> clothes, which at least could not have been
> described as "dowdy". Her thin, straight dark
> hair became an excuse for extravagant indoor
> headgear, which varied from shrill colours by
> day to gold or silver at night.[3]

Brittain could see past appearances, and warmed to the senior student's personality. She recorded that Sayers was kind to freshers and listened to them with great interest. She added that Sayers often appeared to be getting ready for a tea party with her apron and kettle.

Sayers felt herself to be relatively plain of face, but the carefully chosen clothes and her slim, tall figure helped to do justice to her appearance. At Godolphin School a nickname, "Swanny", had referred to her long, slender neck. The beauty of her arms, hands, and voice (both in speaking and singing) were often remarked upon by others over the years.

Sayers was full of anticipation for university life. The fact that neither she nor fellow undergraduates at Somerville would end up with a university degree, no matter how outstanding their scholarly results at the finish, did not seem to perturb her. In that peaceful period before unexpected war, it seemed ordained in the fabric of society that only men could receive degrees, even if they only managed finally to scrape a pass. It was also expected that female students were to be chaperoned when with men that were neither in their family nor covered by a few other exceptions. Somerville College, however, taught their courses to demanding Oxford standards, and the certificates the women gained, though not degrees, would give them far more choice over their futures.[4]

Somerville College had begun as "Somerville Hall" in 1879, one of the earliest women's colleges in the city and, fifteen years later, was renamed "College" instead of "Hall", indicating that the institution would "not only improve the educational status of Somerville in the eyes of the public, but would be understood as implying the desire of [the] Governing Body to raise it above the level of a hall of residence".[5]

It was named after the distinguished Scottish scientist and mathematician Mary Somerville (1780–1872). She had stood up to the resistance, in her time, to women following an academic career, thus providing a model and inspiration for new generations of women. She also demonstrated the connectedness of knowledge in the sciences in a bestselling book for the general reader: *On the Connexion of the Physical Sciences* (1834), which shows affinities with Sayers' own important belief in the connections between different areas of knowledge. Sayers' intellectual development would also share the distinguished scientist's Christian belief as a spur to academic enterprise, and relatedly to female emancipation.[6]

In contrast to the strong historic Anglicanism for over 300 years of most Oxford colleges, Somerville was non-denominational and boasted no chapel. Sayers was anything but superficial. Within the college ethos, she had the freedom among her peers to use her theatrical imagination to try out various positions within her Anglican heritage, ranging from apparent agnosticism to liturgical high church ceremony (a position in which she eventually settled, though never accepting Rome). Though she always would have a strong core of Christian orthodoxy, being deeply appreciative of the creeds, there was to be considerable development, both intellectual and imaginative, in her Christian worldview throughout her life, as she allowed it to be tested by an educated woman's experience.[7]

There are times when Sayers records her thoughts about her beliefs which suggest that, in her undergraduate period, she was for a while agnostic – famously in her letter of March 1914 to her parents. These can equally be read as "What if" speculations as she, quite rightly, considers and worries over the possibility that beliefs she's been taught from childhood will not pass the tests of life itself and may not even be true. In the transition from childhood to adulthood, and periods of trial, it is of course necessary to test faith. This process is a feature of maturing rather than a set agnosticism. There seems no evidence of persistent doubt over a long period that would suggest agnosticism, which itself is a belief that can be questioned. Sayers, significantly, expresses gratitude to G.K. Chesterton, particularly his book, *Orthodoxy,* for help in establishing her faith, which is clearly consistent when considered through the many phases of her complex life. A sense of sin is one aspect of her core belief that persisted in her sensibility.

At the onset of her first year Sayers found it necessary, like numerous other freshers, to be coached for examinations called "Responsions", as a necessary gateway to her degree courses. As well as languages, they included divinity. Although her father had started her on Latin many years before, her enthusiasms had soon become for French and German. Of particular importance to her now, therefore, was to be prepared in Latin and Greek. She was very appreciative of her coach, a Mr Herbert May of Wellington Square in Oxford, who unerringly guided her, she said, through the storms of Latin prose and Greek "Unseens". She noticed him to be the kindest and calmest man of her acquaintance.

Following her own experience, in later years she was to stress the teaching of Latin from very young as part of her *The Lost Tools of Learning*, commenting with amusement that learning Latin should begin as soon as possible, when a child is still growing in a world that in every way is astonishing. Amusingly she suggests that voicing *amo, amas, amat* is as enjoyable to the young child as *eeny, meeny, mineey, mo*.[8]

Very soon into the first term, Sayers' irrepressible energy led her, along with Amphyllis Middlemore,[9] a fellow pupil from Godolphin School who also had attained entry to Somerville, to start an informal club called the "Mutual Admiration Society" (MAS).[10] Others were enthusiastic members from the start. In fact, the society's weekly meetings were arranged by the 1912 freshers: Charis Barnett, Margaret Chubb, Dorothy Rowe, Amphyllis Middlemore, and Sayers herself.[11] New members gradually joined, including from subsequent years' intakes, such as future science-fiction writer Muriel "Jim" Jaeger, and later playwright and distinguished Tudor historian (editor of the six-volume *Lisle Letters*), Muriel St Clair Byrne. Vera Brittain, as a fresher, described the latter in *Chronicles of Youth*, not unkindly, as "the little bright short-haired person with glasses… amusing

& instructive".[12] Some would become lifelong and influential friends of Sayers (Muriel St Clair Byrne, for instance, was to have an important place in directing her toward drama and the theatre). It appears that Sayers was responsible for the club's title of Mutual Admiration Society, pointing out that if they didn't call it that "the rest of the college would".[13]

In one of her works, Barbara Reynolds explains that Sayers was "gregarious" not "solitary" in personality.[14] Given this orientation, the weekly group reflected her love for things read out aloud, and for the give-and-take of boisterous but informed discussion and raised-voice, heartfelt argument, particularly among friends. In this sense she resembled the jovial C.S. Lewis, who became a friend later in life. In some ways, the MAS anticipated Sayers' joy in participating in the Detection Club, established in London in 1930, and other early Oxford groups, such as her Coffee Club and Rhyme Club.

The enjoyment Sayers got from the varied clubs very often centred on language, with the Rhyme Club generating fun and nonsense, as one line was erratically bundled onto another by quick-witted participants. In one party, stories followed on from one development after another like a round robin. (In later life this fun idea led to crime stories broadcast on BBC Radio and then published, where each participating crime writer would follow on, adlibbing from one chapter to another.) Sayers confessed to a *Daily Express* journalist that one of her parties led to an initial inspiration for her first crime novel, not written until some years later: *Whose Body?* At the party (probably uproarious) she found herself suggesting in an unrolling story the discovery of a naked corpse of an unknown person in someone's bath.[15]

Admission to the closed MAS group, which soon became eagerly sought, required reading a piece each supplicant had written for approval by members. Charis Barnett recollected one of Sayers' later offerings as being an imagined conversation between the Magi, who are famed for their appearance in the Gospel of Matthew. This is an extraordinary revelation of the undergraduate's inner thoughts at this time, as a much more mature Sayers many years later would include dialogue of the Magi in her children's book, *The Days of Christ's Coming,* her Nativity BBC broadcast of 1938, *That He Should Come,* and in her follow-up BBC hit radio drama on the life of Christ, *The Man Born to Be King* (1941–42).

From the MAS members that are recorded in Sayers' letters and elsewhere it is obvious that as a result of collective variety of their interests and subjects of study that conversations in their meetings were likely to be wide ranging, and to quickly dip from philosophy or theology to jest. As women they were on the cusp of great and painful changes in society and culture as their top-level educational empowerment opened up, for that time, almost unimaginable opportunities and conflicts. A contemporary Somerville student, Winifred Holtby, would write in later years of women's education that "the burden not only of domestic responsibility but of masculine discouragement lies heavily on the woman student… the conflicting claims of family and professional duties rend her".[16] Their minds, clearly the equal of men's as they followed the rigours of their courses, were fully engaged, despite these conflicts and burdens.

One subject of conversation that was constant is revealed by Vera Brittain. She was younger than Sayers, and never a member of the MAS – though she did belong to another circle of Sayers', her "coffee parties", along with Doreen Wallace, Winifred Holtby (who would become among the Somerville novelists),[17] Aldous Huxley and others. Vera Brittain was familiar of course with undergraduate conversations among Somerville's women at that time. The constant subject was sex. In her *Chronicle of Youth* Vera Brittain's diary records a conversation with a school friend:

Cora [Stoop] & I discussed sex questions
– I propounding my theory, which dawned
upon me when first I knew I loved, that sex
attraction has a threefold nature of spirit, mind
& body just like our whole being, & that we
ought not to despise the physical attraction,
so long as it is the symbol of a spiritual union
also, just because we have it in common with
all creation. Rather, because it is elemental &
fundamental, we should reverence it as one of
the laws of God.[18]

Sayers observed, looking back a few years later, that there must be a reason that the talk of all her friends would centre directly on just one theme. She lamented the fact that the teaching staff seemed incapable of passing on "social wisdom" to their students, that is, wisdom relating to sexuality and the sexes.[19]

In the context of such frank discussions, it is likely that birth control would have been discussed by society members. The bright students of the MAS would be aware of the changes this could make to their lives, in handling work and domestic life. It also could put off the real physical dangers of giving birth, which raised the possibility of a much shorter life. We know that two members – Charis Barnett (later Mrs Charis Frankenburg) and Margaret Chubb – were to become deeply involved in the issue. Charis Frankenburg would write books on birth control and childbearing, while Margaret Chubb, a doctor's daughter, was to become Secretary of the National Birth Control Association. Birth control was to become a vexing issue for Sayers in the 1920s, during and after her friendship with a writer and translator she loved and hoped to marry, and ultimately the issue became traumatic and life changing.[20] During that difficult period, she would turn to Charis Frankenburg for advice on practicalities of birth control methods. Even outside of the Roman Catholic Church, many churchmen in free and state denominations at that time opposed, or were uncertain about, contraception.

A number in the MAS were to become future established writers, but across the board in Somerville College there were enough future novelists in Sayers' generation to be counted by literary scholars as a distinctive movement. Some MAS members are considered to be part of the "Somerville School of Novelists", a title first used by Vera Brittain.[21] Listings of this school vary but the generation of novelists includes Vera Brittain, Dorothy L. Sayers, Muriel Jaeger, Hilda Reid, Sylvia Thompson, Margaret Kennedy, Winifred Holtby, and Doreen Wallace. It seemed almost a new species of woman, the highly educated, that feature in the fictions of the Somerville authors.[22]

Sayers' first biographer, Janet Hitchman, interestingly identifies novelist Doreen Wallace with the work-worn, farming character Catherine Bendick (née Freemantle) in Sayers' mystery novel, *Gaudy Night*. Certainly, there are compelling clues, such as a reference to the demands of rural tithes and hard-hearted "Ecclesiastical Commissioners", a matter over which Sayers and Wallace strongly disagreed.[23] As a former student at the fictional Shrewsbury College, Catherine had stood out at college but had then gone on to marry a farmer and to take on what had become drudgery, weighed down with children, "a Derby winner making shift with a coal-cart". Ironically, a similar phrase was used by Basil Blackwell of Sayers in her brief spell in publishing not long after university: "a race horse harnessed to a plough".[24]

The story goes that Doreen Wallace was peeved over the association with her and the fictional Catherine. She might, however, have been mistaken over Dorothy's intentions in including the character. With perhaps admirable objectivity,

Sayers has Catherine Bendick committed to the life she chose because she has many notions concerning the dignity found in labour. Sayers' theological and social thinking was to focus a great deal on the virtue of work, including its hard demands, and the sacrifice involved, as very much part of the divine image that defines human beings. She did stress, however, that work needed to be appropriately creative to express this image of God without distortion. In *Gaudy Night,* Harriet Vane's friend Catherine had become a tired drudge, rather than being fulfilled by a joy in working, even during toil. The whole idea of the value and nature of work runs strongly through *Gaudy Night.* Catherine is an important and no doubt intentional challenge to Sayers' own work ethic, represented in Harriet Vane, as the novelist tried to balance Catherine's experience with the need for educated women to incorporate their knowledge and gifts in their chosen work.

Doreen Wallace would rue the falling out with Sayers that lay in the distant future. Thinking of her meeting and friendship with Sayers in 1917 after the latter's return to Oxford she remembered how it uplifted her spirit: "Long and slim in those days, small head held alert on slender neck, she loped around Oxford looking for fun.… I have never known anyone so brimful of the energy of a well-stocked mind… and nothing would content her but fact.… Everything she said was a statement, almost an edict."[25] Susan Leonardi points out that Wallace and Sayers were argumentative. She quotes Janet Hitchman: "Dorothy the Christian, back in the fold after her flirtation with agnosticism, and Doreen the unbeliever, neither moving one inch from her stance."[26]

Sayers' colourful sociability and seeming preference for it over the long haul of intense study reveals the dominance of appearance over reality in her college days. It is true that in the final term of her first year she had admitted, in her customary weekly letter to her parents, that the more time she spends in Oxford the more it becomes clear to her that an academic career was not right for her.[27] She was fortunate, however, as she soon realized, to have Miss Mildred Pope as her tutor. By the beginning of her second year, Miss Pope was to report on Sayers' progress: "This term has shown quite unusual quality. She combines with a strong literary appreciation and considerable insight, a real, and rather rare, liking for thoroughness."[28]

Among medieval manuscripts Sayers studied under Mildred Pope were surviving fragments of *The Romance of Tristan and Iseult*, written in the twelfth century in the Anglo-Norman dialect, by someone called Thomas. Sayers' studies were to lead to a growing love of translation, which was to feature strongly in her life and work. She believed that Thomas the writer was either an Englishman or someone who had close links to England. She considered him a poet of rare gifts. Some years after leaving Somerville, when Sayers had shared her translation of *Tristan of Brittany* with Miss Pope for her comments, her former tutor encouraged her to submit a section to a new journal launched by the Modern Language Association, which Sayers had newly joined, probably at Miss Pope's insistence. The translation would be published in full in 1929, establishing Sayers' reputation in the world of scholarship, though she served at no university institution. A notable literary scholar of the time, George Saintsbury, happily provided an introduction for Sayers' translation, in which he declared that we have "one of the most widely disseminated, and even in a way greatest stories of the modern Western World".[29]

Sayers' immersion in the famous love story of Tristan and Iseult prefigures an even deeper attachment to another medieval love story – that of Dante and Beatrice – that was to crown the last years of her work and life. Sayers' mental life clearly was not simply confined to the intellectual pattern of things, but included the romantic and imaginative dimension – an inclusion which might be called the "feeling intellect" or even the *passion* of the intellect.[30]

In reading and studying medieval tales that portrayed romantic love, the ever playful Sayers may have intentionally self-dramatized the longing of Tristan for Iseult, or perhaps, even more, Princess Rigmel's overwhelming desire for Prince Horn in the French *Romance of Horn,* which she would have been familiar with from her exposure to medieval French literature. An important part of student life in Somerville was the Oxford Bach Choir. Many of Sayers' friends, and her younger cousin Margaret Leigh (who started at Somerville after Sayers) sang in it, as did Vera Brittain. It was at rehearsals, in particular, that swooning Sayers exaggerated the drama of romantic longing to the fascination of her fellow students, many of whom could see the attraction of Dr Allen, the choir leader.

Sayers had a strong musical background, of course, due to the inspiration of her father – one-time master of Christ Church Choir, and a minor composer. Part of the attraction of the Bach Choir to Sayers, and other young women, was the charismatic Dr Hugh Allen, later Professor of Music at Oxford. The inaccessibility of Dr Allen, who was married and in his forties, no doubt helped to keep fantasy as fantasy. Sayers was likely to have been piqued by her studies of medieval stories of courtly love that were originally romances of adultery before they were later transformed into romances of marriage, as medievalist C.S. Lewis famously put it.[31] Though Hugh Allen was likely flattered by adulation from his female students, he was content, to all accounts, simply to act out the role of desirable male. Sayers was also perhaps tickled by the reversal of stereotyped roles. In a letter, she humorously describes – as a strip tease – Dr Allen's gradual discarding of some items of clothing while energetically and heatedly conducting the choir.

The music and words, in the social context of the choir was, of course, a far stronger attraction than its flamboyant conductor. Within the sorrows of affliction, Vera Brittain poignantly describes the healing experience of a Bach Choir rehearsal, while anguished by the expectation of a dear family friend's death from meningitis in the second year of war. In the entry for Monday, 8 February 1915, she writes:

> We had a delightful Bach Choir practice tonight.
> It seems to me a strange but certain truth that
> one can enjoy the humour of things so much
> better when one has an underlying sadness.
> All through the evening, especially during the
> solemn words of the *Requiem,* I could not help
> but think of Victor near to death[32] & Edward's
> and Roland's sorrow on his account, yet the
> humour of Dr Allen's temper in the midst of
> a bad cold, & of Miss Sayers gazing at him as
> though she were in church worshipping her
> only God, appealed to me immensely.[33]

Brittain considered that, all in all, Sayers' "realistic sense of humour saved her from becoming wholly ridiculous".[34]

Whether real or largely dramatized for her audience of friends and fellow students, the crush on Dr Hugh Allen was one of several "grand passions" (as one writer on Sayers described it) that the budding scholar demonstrated. Another desirable male over whom Dorothy was briefly awestruck was a student, Maurice Roy Ridley, who would one day be chaplain of Balliol College, as her father had been chaplain at Christ Church. She was love-struck in the style of Dante over Beatrice in thirteenth-century Florence when she heard Ridley, in a charming voice, read his poem on "Oxford" at the Sheldonian Theatre, on the annual occasion of conferral of degrees (conferred to males only at that period, as noted earlier). As well as his degree, Ridley received the prestigious Newdigate Prize of 1913 for his poem. Soon afterwards she wrote to a MAS friend, Catherine "Tony" Godfrey, telling her that she and Charis Barnett became infatuated with him immediately.

Unlike Dante, however, who never forgot Beatrice, Sayers very soon forgot Ridley – well almost! Without realizing it, nearly ten years later, she would be modelling her famous aristocratic sleuth, Lord Peter Wimsey, upon him, even portraying Ridley's features. Over twenty years rolled by, however, before she saw Ridley again, not realizing she had seen him that day in the Sheldonian. This was when she, and another friend from the MAS of bygone days, Muriel St Clare Byrne, were looking out for a suitable actor for Wimsey in a play called *Busman's Honeymoon* (1937) that she and Muriel had scripted together.[35] Sayers was visiting Oxford when she saw again the ideal man. It was the very same Maurice Roy Ridley.

Not everyone was convinced by the idea of Ridley's likeness to Wimsey. While an undergraduate in 1943, Rachel Trickett was tutored for a "term on Shakespeare with Roy Ridley at Balliol, popularly supposed among us to be the original of Lord Peter Wimsey, though, to tell the truth, it had been something of a disappointment".[36]

Sayers had an acute ear for a quality voice. Another's voice that greatly attracted her, but not in an erotic way, was that of G.K. Chesterton, whose book *Orthodoxy,* which she had read while at Godolphin School, had helped her to keep her Christian faith through all the turbulence of early adulthood. Near the end of her life she was to laud Chesterton fervently as a delightful explosion of fresh air for young adults of her time. Rather than defensive and dull, he was adventurous and also wise in conveying Christian polemic.[37]

When Chesterton spoke on "Romance" in Trinity term 1914, at the University Examination School on High Street, Sayers was there, enthralled by his words, his voice still eloquent, sincere and engaging, despite a severe cold. In a letter afterwards to her parents, she wrote that it would be much better if his books were read just as she had heard him speaking. He spoke slowly, and put over insights that really challenged without belligerence, rather having a pleasant manner.[38]

On 7 June of that year, her weekly letter to her parents reported that she heard Chesterton again at the Newman Society meeting, on "Capitalism and Culture". Sayers thought he was especially good when he answered questions after the lecture. It was rumoured that he had just become a Roman Catholic. Sayers hoped not. It would lead, she felt, to fewer books and different ones.[39]

Into Sayers' student world of 1914 came the lengthening shadow of war. Ominous stories in the national newspapers seemed unreal in Oxford. In hindsight, it seems extraordinary that Sayers, along with a fellow Somerville student, Elsie Henderson, planned a long holiday visit to France at the beginning of August. The two travelled to Tours, less than 200 miles south-west of Paris, by cross-channel ferry and train, inevitably accompanied by a chaperone, a friend of Elsie's called Miss Lawrence. When they arrived to chaos, Sayers quickly realized that they were not going to have the seven weeks of carefree holiday they had anticipated. She informed her parents on 2 August of her arrival, and couldn't tell them her plans, as they might have returned home in a week. She assured her parents there was no danger, but that they were essentially within a siege as provisions rapidly dried up through the swift disappearance of transport. All trains and much of local transport (including rustic horses and carts) were commandeered for troops and supplies. The called-up men, prepared by France's compulsory military service, were neatly funnelled to the frontiers to protect France's borders from German invasion. When, the next day, Sayers wrote again to her parents, she put things starkly. The whole thing was like an H.G. Wells novel, with everywhere going to war.

Sayers found herself greatly excited to be there in the middle of things, increasingly aware that England would very quickly also be. Her fluent French, as she read newspapers, listened to the patriotic townspeople, and asked questions, allowed her to grasp the situation. Sayers welcomed the resistance of Belgium after the invasion of Luxembourg. In Tours, she observed men, young and older, bidding farewell to their families. To make matters worse, Elsie fell ill. As soon as the seemingly endless stream of conscripts abated, the trio, with Elsie still recovering, headed for Paris to get a connection to a channel port. Characteristically Sayers had fitted in some holiday ventures, walking along the banks of the River Cher (which made her think of Oxford's rather different Cherwell) and visiting the "beautiful" cathedral and rather hoping she could see other churches, such as St Martin of Tours, complete with his bones.

The three finally arrived at Bluntisham on 25 August. This was instead of Sayers alone, so that Elsie could recuperate at the rectory before heading with Miss Lawrence for her home in Darlington in the north of England. When Sayers returned to Oxford in October for her final year, she discovered it filled with Belgian refugees.

Very aware of the impact of the war, and that it would not be quickly over (as many had hoped), Somerville College released its buildings as a temporary hospital for wounded servicemen, as casualties on the Western Front rapidly grew.

Students received a typed letter from the college, in which was stated:

> In response to an urgent appeal, the Council
> of Somerville College has agreed to allow the
> War Office the use of the College as a military
> hospital for the duration of the War.[40]

The Radcliffe Infirmary at that period was the neighbour of the college on the Woodstock Road, helping the logistics of such a venture. Oriel College in turn, with the great wartime reduction in male student numbers, was able to offer the accommodation around one of its quads – St Mary's, known as the Skimmery quad – for Somerville students. The offer was accepted, and though this meant upheaval and a lot of adjustments, it did mean however that Somerville was now a presence within the large cluster of the university proper. It felt somehow that the college was more part of the university, at least in spirit, even though it was, like the other women's colleges, isolated by not being able to have awards of university degrees. In keeping with the climate of chaperoning, which echoed the quarantine of the young women, the archway connecting the quad "with the rest of the college was scrupulously bricked up", later recorded a first year student, Sayers' cousin Margaret Leigh.[41]

The move of Somerville students to Oriel College took place with the minimum of disruption, and Sayers enjoyed her new location. Oriel's all-male Junior Common Room – the old hall of St Mary's – had become Somerville's dining hall, and a pleasant library was given over for the occupying women's common room. Sayers' room overlooked the High Street, exactly opposite to the university church of St Mary's. With more shelves and cupboards on which to place things than her Somerville room, Sayers felt more comfortable. Having become Bicycle Secretary, one of her greatest challenges was imposing order on the chaotic bike parking. She soon had a reputation for strictness, imposing fines for wrong parking, the proceeds of which went to the now high-profile British Red Cross. The vacated Somerville College was quickly turned into a hospital, with some students volunteering to work there. All were now aware of the growing list of casualties, and many had brothers, uncles, or other relations on the Western Front. Many students felt an overwhelming pressure to leave, in favour of war work, so much so that the government as well as the college argued that it was more important for now and the future for women to pursue higher education, given their indispensable and valued contribution to society.[42]

Barely had Sayers and her friends settled into the college's temporary new home when, alongside study for final examinations, planning began for the Going-Down Play for Sayers' year, a traditional performance for the period between finals and results. MAS members and others were involved in all aspects, script writing and plot, cast, creation of the music-hall-style songs, music, production, and direction. College and some university staff were willingly drawn into what was a light-hearted fun event, even if it was only to lend clothes to the all-female cast, as Dr Hugh Allen did for Sayers, his impersonator. She would use the clothes in the Going-Down Play to powerful effect. In Vera Brittain's words, "she caricatured her idol with triumphant accuracy and zest".[43] A photograph captured her in mid-flight in her role, perfectly echoing a cartoon of the time of Sir Hugh exuberantly conducting the Bach Choir.

The play was titled *Pied Piping, or the Innocents Abroad*. A number of the final year students contributed to it, as well as performing in it. Dorothy Rowe (who would go on to found the Bournemouth Palace Court Theatre)[44] had a leading role, along with Amphyllis Middlemore, in stage managing, and Sayers was both Musical Director and leader of the cast as the Pied Piper, Dr H.P. Rallentando. While the stage managers cleverly moved the audience around the Skimmery (St Mary) quad as scenes changed, Sayers soon left no one in doubt that the Piper was modelled upon the bombastic Dr Hugh Allen. The action has the Piper leading the audience abroad into "Never Land". The anonymous plot summary of the occasion reads:

> The students about to take schools [final examinations] are in despair because their tutors and examiners are constantly making new discoveries and discrediting traditional views of the subjects they have studied. The Piper... leads them to the Never Land where the researchers and experts are confronted with defunct celebrities – Alfred the Great, Shakespeare etc. – who confound their critics. The latter do not enjoy themselves and ask to be taken back to Oxford, but the Piper says this is impossible. They themselves have now become defunct and younger scholars are already engaged in controversy about them....[45]

As well as laughing at herself in caricaturing Dr Allen, her ostentatious crush on the musician being so well known, Sayers also addressed many of her failings or habits that she knew irked fellow students in a song for the Piper in Gilbert and Sullivan style that she may have written. This effectively transformed her quirks from the student grumbles to stand-up comedy. "The Bicycle Secretary's Song" draws upon "I've Got a Little List", from *The Mikado*. After singing about the careless bicycle pests, and her strict regime of imposed order, Sayers moves on in the "little list" of her blemishes that have imposed upon Somerville life. "I've made a little list," she sings in her strong voice, which includes those who argue loudly at night, those strolling at breakfast time in silk nightgowns, or those whistling "Bach or Verdi" while walking across the quad, not forgetting the blighters who drop catalogues or whisper in the Bodleian library. The "little list" goes on, no doubt to increasing laughter of recognition. The refrain is: "They'll none of them be missed", alluding to the actual poignant finality of going-down from the college.[46]

Vera Brittain remembers the play closing with all the cast singing together a piece about Oxford by Dorothy Rowe, written to the tune of "John Peel", and ending with the lines:

> For we've had a good time,
> And there's more ahead.
> And we're all going down in the morning.[47]

After the formidable and compulsory *viva voce*, following her final examinations, Sayers was awarded the distinction of a first class honours in modern (that is, medieval) French to take with her into a world full of uncertainty for any highly educated woman at that time.

She characteristically wrote a poem for her friends after leaving, and sent them handwritten copies. It ends by blessing the "enchanted town" she loved and the new adventures of her friends.

4

POETRY, PUBLISHING, AND A TRY AT TEACHING
(1916–20)

"It was like harnessing a racehorse to a plough."
Basil Blackwell[1]

The distinguished new graduate Dorothy L. Sayers clearly was not convinced that an academic life was for her, even if she were to become able to impart social as well as intellectual knowledge to students she could imagine she would have. In her bones she felt that, while she loved researching, there was in her a nascent desire to write publishable poetry, also to translate verse, and even to write stories. The genre of looked-down-upon detection, mystery and, horror books (as she was to group them) was already starting to tickle her attention.[2] Somehow she could make herself free to be a gregarious woman whose work was writing, if she could be determined enough to make enough money to support herself.

Following the Somerville finals, friends – from the Mutual Admiration Society, as well as others – were going off in a number of directions. Some were taking roads less travelled rather than simply adopting the few predetermined routes considered right and proper for women, even if it meant being a farmer on often tough terrain – as were later writers Margaret Leigh, Sayers' cousin, who graduated the following year, and Doreen Wallace, who graduated several years after.

Dorothy Rowe returned to her home town, and was an inspired and memorable teacher of English in Bournemouth High School (renamed Talbot Heath School in 1935) until 1957, as well as continuing her interest in stagecraft by directing in and transforming a local theatre. One school pupil remembered: "By a change of expression she could be anything – Lady Macbeth – Ophelia – Falstaff – Abraham Lincoln – or even a pussy cat."[3] Sayers would call upon her help with any form of drama in which she was involved, whether school plays or film scripts, and often would visit her in Bournemouth in her early years as a developing writer. She could always rely upon Dorothy Rowe being interested in productions of her plays.

Charis Barnett had been brought up as a Christian, not knowing until later she was in fact Jewish in origin. She responded to an appeal for volunteers from the Quakers and went to nurse in France after her brother Donald was killed in battle. Upon her return Charis married her Jewish second-cousin, Sydney Frankenberg, who encouraged her work in Salford promoting birth control, writing books and articles, and educating over child rearing. With a talent for organizing, she set up Manchester, Salford and District Mothers' Clinic and much else.[4]

Margaret Chubb, like Charis Barnett, pursued a lifelong commitment to issues of family planning. In the last year of the war she met Cambridge-educated Geoffrey Pyke, a brilliant and highly eccentric journalist, spy, innovator, financial speculator, and scientist. He had become a celebrity through escaping from a German internment camp. Deeply attracted, she married him within months. After his suicide in 1948, his *The Times* obituary judged: "The death of Geoffrey Pyke removes one of the most original if unrecognized figures of the present century."[5] Margaret Chubb's name is highlighted today in the Margaret Pyke Trust, a charity internationally supporting medical education in sexual and reproductive health.

Immediately after graduation, Amphyllis Middlemore became – according to Godolphin School *Old Girls* [sic] *News* – "organising secretary under the Staffordshire County Council for their thrift scheme throughout the county". This included "local instruction in cooking and economical house-keeping, and in mother craft, and also a system of labour exchange, chiefly for agricultural work [it was thought]". Her work entailed "much writing and going about visiting, in the various districts, and arranging meetings and committees".[6]

Catherine Godfrey elected to teach English, getting a post in Blackheath, London. Under the pressures she encountered as a new teacher, she had to give up after suffering a breakdown.

Muriel Jaeger had a fourth year to complete in her studies at Somerville, and in later years was a pioneer in science-fiction writing, as well as an author of non-fiction, *Sisyphus: Or, the Limits of Psychology* (1929). Her first fiction, *The Question Mark* (1926), was published by Leonard and Virginia Woolf, as was *The Man with Six Senses* (1927). The first, which undermines the utopian vision of writers like William Morris, Edward Bellamy, and H.G. Wells, may have influenced Aldous Huxley's *Brave New World* (1932).[7]

Muriel St Clare Byrne was also completing her studies at Somerville, and would graduate two years after Sayers in 1917. She would become a specialist historical researcher, focusing upon the Tudor period, and notable for her fifty years' research, leading to the publication of the six-volume *The Lisle Papers*. Her interest in theatre took her to lecturing at the Royal Academy of Dramatic Art and becoming a governor at the Royal Shakespeare Theatre. She was also important in encouraging Sayers' long interest in drama in the thirties, in co-writing the play *Busman's Honeymoon*, upon which the final Lord Peter Wimsey novel was based.

Always a fervent letter-writer, Sayers enjoyed keeping in touch with her friends. Her letters record her meeting up with them as often as she could. A first occasion, soon after going down from Somerville, was when she invited a few of her friends – Catherine Godfrey, Dorothy Rowe, and Muriel Jaeger – to the rectory at Bluntisham during the summer vacation, before they went their separate ways. They had a few cheerful days together in late June. There was another get-together, this time in London, where Sayers, and Catherine Godfrey, joined Charis Barnett in her house. They made themselves comfortable on the floor around a gas-stove without gas, and talked well into the night, as if they were still at Somerville. There was no gas as a precaution against German Zeppelins, which had dropped bombs a number of times on the capital. While there, Sayers took the opportunity to shop for a coat and skirt, appreciating the help in this of Charis and her sister-in-law. She also experienced escalators for the first time. Modern life in London districts like Battersea, Bloomsbury, and Hammersmith would one day come with familiarity into her novels including *Whose Body?* and *Murder Must Advertize,* and into her short stories like "Nebuchadnezzar".[8]

Sayers had returned to Bluntisham upon leaving Oxford with her mind rather in turmoil over her next step. Life in the Fen village couldn't be in greater contrast to life in her favoured city. The visit there from her friends that June had eased the wound somewhat. She told them of her initial plan to go as a nurse to France. She felt that it would be good to do something useful, even though she was very aware of her fear of the horrors and all-consuming toil. In fact, the French Red Cross turned her down, despite her mastery of French, as she was too young, being under twenty-three. She was also wondering if she could receive nurse training at the Radcliffe Infirmary, or teach in a boys' school, where there was a need for female staff. She had a brief respite from having to make a decision when the librarian, Vera Farnell, invited her to help temporarily at the Somerville College library during the autumn term of 1915.

Her mind was still very much upon Oxford, which was linked to her urge to write poetry, which she did in a variety of sometimes complex structures over that summer and autumn. She had heard of two projects from the Oxford booksellers, Blackwell's, which had ventured into publishing in 1879. The founder's son, Basil Blackwell, a graduate of Merton College, had established an annual poetry collection in 1913 called *Oxford Poetry*. His aim was to find talented young poets and give them a platform. With the same aim, he had also initiated an ambitious poetry series called *Adventurers All*, each featuring a single author, eight of which had appeared the year before. One of them had been written by Aldous Huxley (future author of *Brave New World*), who was a year younger than Sayers, and studying at Balliol College, Oxford. Both projects appealed to Sayers, and she submitted "Lay", based upon a type of medieval lyric, or lay, often involving adventures and the supernatural, which in her case was constructed as twelve interconnected poems. The lay featured the beauty and imaginative appeal of her fond city, Oxford, with one section featuring Tristan and Iseult, which was accepted by its editors for the 1915 volume.[9] The editors of *Oxford Poetry 1915* were G.D.H. Cole and T.W. Earp (called by Sayers' contemporary at Oxford, J.R.R. Tolkien, the "original twerp",[10] the term deriving from his name). Along with Sayers' first publication, the volume included a poem by Dorothy Rowe, Tolkien's first published poem, "Goblin Feet", and a poem by one of the latter's closest friends, G.B. Smith, destined to die in action the next year.

Bowing to the inevitable, having visited a cousin, Raymond Sayers, and his wife in Great Yarmouth, and Dorothy Rowe in Bournemouth, Sayers soon found herself teaching. She had travelled north to Kingston-upon-Hull early in January 1916, to become French mistress at the Girls' High School. Hull was more interesting a city than she expected and her accommodation pleasing, though she found some of the city "ugly and *dreadfully* dirty" from soot and other pollution.[11] Westbourne Avenue was tree-lined, as its name suggests, with the houses set back some distance from the road. Her house, number 80, was near to a public park. The school was then located in Park Street, less than one and a half miles away, and years later moved to Tranby Croft, Anlaby, in Hull. Sayers was to become one of a number of authors (predominantly poets) having an association with the city, which include Philip Larkin, Andrew Motion, Stevie Smith, J.R.R. Tolkien, and Andrew Marvell.

Although, as she later confessed, Sayers never took to teaching, she threw herself into her duties as French mistress. With her boundless creativity, she set out to repair stunted progress in classes that had been set too much on rote learning, with little awareness of meaning. Her discovery in childhood of the connectedness of knowledge never was to desert her. Before long, some of her pupils under her direction were attempting to act out French dramas, some of which they composed themselves. They even put on a classic seventeenth-century French play, Molière's *Les Précieuses Ridicules* (*The Pretentious Young Ladies*), with the ticket money going to the Red Cross. Molière ridicules the pretentious language and manners deemed fashionable at that period in France.

Sayers didn't confine herself to her teaching of French, but also set up a school choir, which she led, no doubt, with humour and infectious enthusiasm. In addition, she joined the Hull Vocal Society, along with a friendly science teacher. She and Miss Biggs also searched for the "highest" Anglican church they could find, as she became more progressively Anglo-Catholic. Sayers found the headmistress affable, and would join her in visiting the theatre and cinema. As background to her full life in Hull, however, were bombing raids by Zeppelins, which Sayers described as "hell", especially when she was shaken by seeing her landlady reduced to terror by one raid, confessing in a letter that she had never before seen such brutal and sheer animal fear.[12]

Late in the spring term of 1916, Sayers was delighted to hear that Blackwell's had accepted her collection of poems, *Op. I,* for publication in the *Adventurers All* series. The meaning of the term is ambiguous: was it signalling her first opus, or did it mean her first collection of Oxford poetry? Whichever, it was to be her first publication of a book, reinforcing her choice to aim for a writing life. As the summer vacation approached, she wondered how the free time could best be devoted to her poetry. At the beginning of August she contacted Cambridge University Library, in the city centre, for permission to use it. She explained her interest in early French romances, and was granted a temporary reader's ticket. As a reader, she could consult rare manuscripts and books, but not borrow any books. Her plan was to follow up on the work she had engaged in as a student under her brilliant tutor, Miss Mildred Pope. In particular, in Cambridge she had access to texts of the medieval romances, *The Song of Roland* and *The Romance of Tristan and Iseult,* as well as scholarly work on them. In the future she would publish highly regarded translations of the two works. The library was convenient for Bluntisham, just twenty miles away, though the Cambridge railway station was some distance from the centre.

Later that year, Sayers prepared a lecture in Hull on the Celtic theme of "Other World" journeys, which revealed the affinity her imagination and feelings had with medieval images of reality, encompassing this and other worlds. Her thinking is likely to have been stimulated by her perusal of medieval French writings, some shaped by Celtic themes, at the Cambridge University Library. Her lecture, given at a November meeting of the Association of Assistant Mistresses, was intriguingly called "The Way to the Other World". Sayers speculated about the presence of the eternal in the temporal. She saw the "Other World" as a definite place, yet our world, and the land of fairy, exist together upon an identical small piece of ground. She put it down to what the eye sees. Going from earth to the fairy realm, she speculated, is like passing from our time to the eternal. Around the period of her lecture, a critically ill J.R.R. Tolkien had survived the Battle of the Somme in France and, shortly after, recovering in England, he was in the early stages of the creation of Middle-earth which would lead to the publication of his *The Lord of the Rings* nearly half a century later, in time for Sayers to be able to read it and enjoy it before her death, when she had already become familiar by then with his affinitive views on the fairy tale.

Her conception of other worlds at this time give a foretaste of her later discovery of the great Italian poet Dante and his love for Beatrice. They could have been written by either C.S. Lewis or J.R.R. Tolkien, both her contemporaries and both drawn to the world of fairy and romance (Tolkien was born in 1892, the year before Sayers, and Lewis, five years her junior, in 1898). A similar world outlook can be discovered (as it was by both Lewis and Tolkien) in the nineteenth-century poet, novelist, and fantasy-writer George MacDonald, in his fiction, and in his essays "The Imagination: Its Functions and its Culture" (1867) and "The Fantastic Imagination" (1882). Changes in outlook and consciousness, captured by and caused by glimpses of an "Other World", were at the very heart of the thinking of

MacDonald, and key members of the Inklings: Lewis, Tolkien, Charles Williams, and Owen Barfield. They, too, like Sayers, were concerned with the presence of the eternal in the temporal.[13]

Sayers' stint in Hull would soon be over. She had discussed her prospects with her father over the Christmas holidays of 1916, before returning in the new year for the spring term. Henry Sayers had wanted his daughter to stay at Oxford for a fourth year, which would have stretched his finances. However, he had been offered a much better paid living as rector at Christchurch, a little further north in the Fen country, and had spoken to Basil Blackwell about the possibility of her being an apprentice at the publisher's. This would mean him putting down a sum of £100 pounds to Blackwell's, which enabled them to pay Sayers a small weekly sum of £2. Henry Sayers' approach paid off, and his daughter could imagine herself at Blackwell's, in a bookish world, and in her beloved city, where she would be able to greet for herself the familiar Oxford landmarks like Skimmery quad and Tom Tower instead of having to ask Muriel Jaeger to greet them on her behalf. She would rejoin the Bach Choir. Always a researcher, she spent some time in that last term in Hull at a friendly local printers, learning some of the working procedures, which would likely have included hot metal typesetting of text and preparing photos for printing, the production of proofs, and correction symbols used by editors and proofreaders.

Sayers' apprenticeship with Blackwell's started at the beginning of May 1917, with her finding accommodation at 17, Longwall Street, from where she could contemplate the Magdalen College deer park from her rented rooms, with the better view from upstairs. She quickly connected with Muriel St Clare Byrne, who was completing her final year at Somerville College, and soon had a social life again, with coffee parties, a Rhyme Club, other partying, choir singing, high church ceremony, and rowing and punting on the Rivers Isis (Thames) and Cherwell. She came to know Doreen Wallace,[14] a student who would become a well-known novelist, and who, like her, was tall and slim, fiercely intellectual, and liked a good argument (such as her unbelief versus Sayers' Christianity). She could cope with Sayers' hearty-voiced performance of the hymn "Fling Wide the Gates! The Saviour Waits!" while marching along Oxford's High Street.[15] Doreen Wallace remembered sharing the fun of the Rhyme Club, "one minute to produce the rhyming line, no matter whether sense or nonsense".[16] Among visitors to the club were Siegfried Sassoon (who was convalescing from his war wounds in the temporary hospital at Somerville) and literary brothers Osbert and Sacheverell Sitwell.[17] The coffee parties were attended over time by the likes of Aldous Huxley, T.W. Earp, Vera Brittain, Winifred Holtby, Margaret Irwin, the Sitwells, and later Eric Whelpton after he returned to Oxford.[18] Whelpton had been invalided out of the army, and returned from the Front in May 1918 to continue his studies at Hertford College.

Eric Whelpton was to become an important presence in this period of Sayers's life. Janet Hitchman, Sayers' first biographer, was convinced after conversations with Doreen Wallace that both Wallace and Sayers were attracted to Whelpton.[19] Like the as yet unknown Lord Peter Wimsey, Eric Whelpton had known many women who had fallen for him. Whelpton at that time, as he makes clear in his autobiographical *The Making of a European* (1974), had no wish at that youthful season for a permanent relationship, and claimed he was not particularly attracted to academic women. Both Whelpton and Doreen Wallace had rooms for a time along Bath Place, a beautiful cul-de-sac off Holywell Street. Bath Place was very near Sayers' accommodation in Longwall Street, and she eventually moved to three-room accommodation there (at number 5, in the floor above Whelpton).[20] A wonderful name-dropper, the highly sociable Whelpton may not have been attracted to, but he certainly enjoyed the association with, the highly intelligent likes of Sayers and Wallace, as well as Vera Brittain, Winifred Holtby, and Margaret Irwin.

Among these remarkable women of Oxford, Sayers had given up her well-paid teaching post in Hull in order to take a year's apprenticeship in publishing, a gamble befitting her vision of a life in books. Though her social life was important to her as she mixed with literary friends, she was very aware of the importance of the publishing work giving her a sense of purpose. However, she became despondent over a lack of direction in her return to Oxford life, as she balanced her work routine and social life, and also carried the burden of health issues like appendicitis, German measles, and a mild version of the killer Spanish influenza. Sayers also suffered from her propensity to fall for ill-chosen, undependable men who had been moulded by the turmoil of rapid cultural and social changes of the time.

Sayers was the young Basil Blackwell's very first editorial assistant. Blackwell's agreement was to teach Sayers everything there was to know about publishing. She made it clear from the onset that she was "Dorothy L. Sayers", the "L" of course being for her mother's maiden name, "Leigh". A publishing house could understand this, with their constant need for precision. In the official history "of a Family Firm", *Blackwell's 1879–1979,* we are told that Sayers arrived at Broad Street "a tall, very slim young woman dressed in a formal blue serge costume with informal yellow stockings".[21] She became endeared to a small room allocated to her high in the Blackwell's shop, with its aerial view of "the caesars", the busts in front of the Sheldonian Theatre, where, unanticipated by her, Sayers would in three years' time be one of the first women to receive an Oxford University degree.

Although her boss thought highly of Sayers' intelligence and wit, he did have reservations about some of her opinions. Basil Blackwell once recalled a crucifix that Sayers had on her desk, and how she would express her religious beliefs in a way he found repelling. Nevertheless, he did remember a softer and kind side to her also.

Sayers was hardworking, attending to her allotted duties intended to teach all that was involved in the business of publishing. As Basil Blackwell observed his apprentice, he slowly came to the conclusion that her intelligence and creativity were being underused. It seems he felt perhaps that he needed someone more slow, steady, and business orientated; someone less imaginative and ready with a routine opinion. Then, in April 1919, Sayers found herself under big financial pressures. Her arrangement with Blackwell's had changed to undertaking only piece-work with them. In fact, she was no longer an apprentice with the prospect of being a future publisher with Blackwell's. She had been removed from this position. It was little consolation that she could take on other freelance work (such as coaching of students and freelance journalism). The honest Basil Blackwell recalled: "At the end of some three [sic] years I had to tell her that it was not fair to expect her to become a steady efficient publisher. It was like harnessing a racehorse to a plough."[22]

During her apprenticeship, Sayers had edited, along with other editors, *Oxford Poetry 1917, Oxford Poetry 1918,* and *Oxford Poetry 1919,* contributing a single poem in the 1917 and 1918 volumes, and three poems in the 1919 volume. Blackwell's also published her book, *Catholic Tales and Christian Songs* in 1918. "Catholic" in the title refers to universally held Christian beliefs, not to a denomination, and is influenced by G.K. Chesterton.[23] *Catholic Tales* introduced Sayers to controversy, which would be a feature of many of her Christian writings, ironically because of their orthodox and realistic stance, and their delight in dogma. Like Chesterton, Sayers had a strong comic sense, which an over-pious, indignant reader could easily miss. Her writing affirmed Chesterton for whom orthodoxy, he wrote, "has been one whirling adventure; and in my vision the heavenly chariot flies thunderingly through the ages, the dull heresies sprawling and prostrate, the wild truth reeling but erect".[24]

Blackwell's list of new publications rather cryptically pointed out that Sayers' poems would astonish the reader with their "intense conviction", appearing on the surface to some as blasphemy, but their words were actually "inspired" in three equal measures by the New Testament, the Church Fathers, and her contemporary, G.K. Chesterton. Because of objections to it, Sayers explained the poetry book to her parents in a letter, adding that Basil Blackwell was very enthusiastic about it. She pointed out to them that while some readers considered the book delightful, others denounced it as blasphemy. In fact, the book was meant to be reverent, as she considered an energetic expression of faith can be. Christ was the subject of the poems. From what she wrote in the book, and what she said about the poems, it is evident that they carried her belief in Christ, which would underlie her future writings.

Sayers was certainly lively as well as reverent, and relevant in a rapidly changing post-war world. Religious emotion is evident in the very existence of these poems – the Sayers who is sometimes portrayed (even by herself) as distant from feeling and emotion in her Christian beliefs isn't really evident in the author of *Catholic Tales and Christian Songs,* even given the prominence of stylistic experimentation.

The period of *Catholic Tales* does however indicate Sayers' sometimes turbulent thinking as she left her youth behind, and as she formed more of the foundations of her future faith, which, as it grew, would be tested in difficult ways. Her biographer,

Ralph E. Hone, isolates one important area. Between 1918 and 1919, Sayers seemed to be struggling between her religion and her physical sensuality. This conflict did not appear to resolve itself.

One literary objection to her book brought in the sympathetic poet, mystic, and writer Charles Williams, who in later years would have a great and dramatic impact upon her and become a solid friend.[25] Theodore Maynard was a Roman Catholic poet who had reviewed Charles Williams' collection, *Poems of Conformity,* very harshly. At first he accused him of being a "Satanist", saying the poetry "has come hot from hell", an accusation he later withdrew. Maynard also reviewed Sayers' *Catholic Tales and Christian Songs.*[26] This, he thought, reduced Christianity down to paganism. In response, Sayers had the idea of persuading her friend Muriel Jaeger to write to the periodical that had carried Maynard's review under assumed names, initiating a "scrumptious" debate. One real reader, a poet, who wrote in pointed out that Maynard's "patronising clericalism" had been already displayed toward Charles Williams, "whose truly noble poetry he vilified from the same viewpoint". Williams joined in with a reply, deftly affirming both Maynard and Sayers. He said that he had liked "most" of *Catholic Tales* and admired in particular her poem "The Mocking of Christ". He added that the review had made him reread the *Catholic Tales,* after which "he liked it more". Sayers and Muriel quickly tired of the joke and left the "Maynard Controversy" to die an inglorious death. Maynard and Williams became friends, and fully affirmed each other's work, an indirect effect of Sayers' playfulness.[27]

The ending of Sayers' apprenticeship at Blackwell's coincided with Eric Whelpton's now established presence on the Oxford scene. Though Maurice Roy Ridley was one day to be a model for Lord Peter Wimsey, Whelpton had some Wimseyan characteristics that attracted Sayers. In fact, Whelpton's *The Making of a European* reveals that he was convinced by friends that he was the original of Lord Peter. He had met Sayers during her time with the publisher and shortly after his return to Oxford from wartime France in May 1918. He remembered that she had been kind to him in a sort of maternal way. He felt her friendship was undeserved as he was intellectually inferior although mature in life experience. Whelpton failed to notice that Sayers, and also it seems Doreen Wallace, had fallen in love with him. When Sayers moved into Bath Place, close to Whelpton's rooms there, he and she rarely visited each other, but they met often at coffee parties, where the talk was about books he had not read, but intended to.[28]

Whelpton, who had grown up in France and was bilingual, heard shortly after the war's end that the headmaster of a notable boarding-school, Ecole des Roche close by Verneuil-sur-Avre, Normandy, was seeking a part-time English Master for the summer term. Though the pay was poor, Whelpton had a disability pension, which meant he would be comfortably off taking up the post. While there he created an agency for arranging exchange visits of English and French schoolboys. He found he needed a bilingual assistant. When Sayers wrote to him enquiring if he knew of any work going in France, he offered his friend the job. She wondered how to explain the employment to her parents, and decided that the best course was to invite Eric Whelpton to the rectory in Christchurch, on his next visit to England, to let them meet him.

Eric Whelpton passed the test, assuring father and mother that he and Sayers would be living in different houses at the school, and were unlikely to see much of each other out of office hours. He also pointed out that his affections were elsewhere. Both parents knew, however, that Sayers had turned down an unsuitable suitor (she had no feelings for him) even though he was rooted to an Anglican college in Oxford, St Edmund's, as Vice-Principal, and had cast-iron prospects. Leonard Hodgson was to become none other than the Regius Professor of Divinity at Oxford, and Canon of Christ Church, who came to agree with the Archbishop of Canterbury that Sayers should be offered an honorary award of Doctor of Divinity.

At this time Sayers appeared to be certain of her wishes, and not impressionable, and at that time was always keeping her parents posted about affairs of the heart. Although Eric Whelpton was never to read *The Nine Tailors*, which appeared years later, he confidently stated (based on the opinions of friends) that the setting of Christchurch and its rectory provided inspiration for the novel. Had he read it, he was likely to have seen Revd Venables, a central character in the story, in Henry Sayers.

Sayers made her own way by ferry and train to Ecole des Roche, taking her bicycle as advised by Whelpton. The two wheels allowed her to explore the flat Normandy countryside, rather like the familiar fenland of her youth, and richly endowed with woodland. The bicycle was also convenient for getting into nearby Verneuil. At the school she shared an office with Whelpton and proved to be thorough and able with the work of setting up and often accompanying school exchanges between Ecole des Roche and English boys' boarding schools. In fact, after a time, Sayers could have taken over the agency.

Perhaps partly due to her efficiency there was plenty of time for both Eric Whelpton and Sayers to pursue their own interests. Whelpton was rather scathing over the time Sayers would spend devouring detective and mystery stories, as well as horror literature, all of which she saw as related. He obviously thought of them as trash, and below him as a highly educated reader. He could little imagine that she was using her great gifts for research in thoroughly acquainting herself with a genre that had great potential as a worthy form of novel, as well as a lucrative source of income for an aspiring self-sufficient author. She tried – and failed – to draw Whelpton into the project, telling him of several Oxford friends who were enthusiastic fellow-researchers.

Whelpton suffered health problems that had been exacerbated by his wartime experience. Polio was involved, but also symptoms which might today be termed as post-traumatic stress disorder. Sayers tried to comfort him through his fainting fits and seizures in a manner he described as "maternal", describing occasions when he would lay his brilliantined head on her knees, sobbing. There is perhaps something of Whelpton's emotional wounding in Sayers' creation of Lord Peter Wimsey, who became an iconic wounded-hero detective, a victim of his experience in the First World War.

Sayers, deeply in love with Whelpton, was patient with his emotional and physical weaknesses. After all, she had been willing to contemplate serving as a nurse to the war-wounded. In the end, on a visit to London, the ex-soldier fell in love with a beautiful woman sitting near him in a theatre, then tracked her down through an advertisement in *The Times*. When they met up, Whelpton asked Frances to marry him without remembering to ask her surname. The divorcee immediately accepted the bold proposal, not telling him that she was dying. Frances was less and less able to spend time with her persistent lover because of her condition, and then she abruptly expired.[29]

Despite the chance to take over the pupil-exchange agency at Ecole des Roche, Sayers decided to return to England, and to London in particular – her feelings in a desperate state. Her sense of work as vocation, and the intellectual and imaginative pull of writing, translating, as well as the strong appeal of Christian dogma, steered her through, however, with a brave heart. She could draw encouragement from the fact that Oxford

University had decided to award degrees to women, following the passing of a bill called the "Women's Statute" by Parliament in February 1920, allowing the granting of university degrees.[30] Sayers quickly paid the due fees and pushed to join the first group from the Oxford women's colleges to receive them.

On 14 October 1920, a warm and sunny day, Sayers and fellow graduates were granted both their Oxford BA and MA degrees on the same day – an unprecedented event – in the Sheldonian Theatre, opposite the familiar Blackwell's bookshop on Broad Street. Usually students received their MA after simply waiting for a period and then paying a fee. Before the annual awarding of university degrees that day to men and women, there was a special ceremony in which the principals of the women's colleges, now Oxford University colleges, received their degrees. After male university students received theirs, there was enthusiastic cheering before seven chosen graduates from each women's college were awarded degrees. Sayers and Muriel St Clare Byrne were among the "Somerville seven".[31]

In the ceremony the following year, remaining Somerville graduates were presented with their Oxford University degrees, including Charis Barnett, now Charis Frankenburg. She had taken along her young son to share the occasion, which proved a challenge for the Vice-Chancellor in his robes. A history of family life in the twentieth century records that Charis' son "announced in such a loud voice that he had a nicer dressing gown than the Vice-Chancellor's, *and* green pyjamas, that the Vice-Chancellor had him removed".[32]

Dorothy L. Sayers, MA, had travelled back to London after the ceremonies – London a relative haven for work in a depressed post-war economy – to seek her fortune, or at least the minimum necessary for rent and survival. Her father would send her money to help when he could. In an ebullient letter to her mother a little over two months later she disclosed that she had been visited with an idea for a crime story. It starts with an overweight lady discovered lifeless in a bath, wearing only her pince-nez. Her adornment opens up a question of why wear it in her bath? When the novel is finished and published, readers would discover that there are many more questions, such as, why is the body in someone else's bath? Actually, the corpse in the fully developed novel is chosen by Sayers to be a man, who is importantly revealed to be uncircumcised, when the suspected victim of the murder is a Jewish financier.

The body found in the bath was a seed of her first mystery story, *Whose Body?* which would appear in 1923 in the US, with a British edition later that year.

But why did Sayer' very first work of fiction appear in America before it appeared in Britain? The answer lies in a passionate but unfulfilled and doomed love affair that would tear Sayers' heart apart.

5

An Accidental Birth and Complex Domesticity (1921–26)

The delight in listening to stories is as natural
to human nature as the delight in looking at
the dancing and miming out of which drama
arose. That it exists unimpaired is shown in
the vogue of the detective novel.

Somerset Maugham, *The Summing Up*[1]

As 1921 began, Sayers was in her twenty-eighth year, and
precariously living in London. She had been desperately in
love with Eric Whelpton, to no avail, though he had admired
the prettiness of her hands, neck, and shoulders, "good"
legs and ankles, and found her generally sweet-tempered and
comfortingly maternal; this was even though she was, to him,
a bit devilish.[2] Sayers now needed work at least to cover her
outgoings in London to pay for her determination to write. She
had two published poetry books to her name. She was quickly
picking up a formidable knowledge of books of detection,
mystery, and horror, her powerfully analytical mind tracing
a definition of a common genre for these three categories of
stories.[3] All the time, she was making sense of the pattern in
which she herself was made: a pattern to cover her powerful,

scholarly intellect, her wide-ranging imagination, and her intense emotions. She was getting to know herself, and felt that each of the aspects of her self somehow needed to live and breathe. Her belief system told her that as a human being she was the equal of any other human, whether male or female, rich or poor, in work or out of work. She longed for community, for proper fulfilment of her unmistakable bodily desires, whether culinary or sexual, for intellectual engagement, and for expression of her literary, poetic, and theatrical imagination. Music remained an important and immensely enriching part of her life; she would spend part of her meagre income on a viola or a fiddle or attending concerts.

By 1921 Sayers was Oxford-educated and degree-bearing, greatly talented, but currently out of steady, full-time work, emotionally wounded by a failure of love, and a person some would label a feminist who had wanted a man who was suitable for her, which of course is not a contradiction. With such a man she could have set the world alight, she revealed in a letter to a former lover several years later.[4] The early years of the 1920s were to be a time of severe trial for the complex person called Dorothy Leigh Sayers.

London had a gravitational pull for educated women who were on new ground. Sayers knew herself well enough not to go for an academic career in Oxford or Cambridge, or for a life of school teaching, or for the milieu of publishing. She had to support herself in order to write, or to be able to go about translating medieval texts, or perhaps even to be able to give an occasional scholarly lecture in a distant location. At that time she hardly knew where or how to start. This newcomer to the great city, however, had women friends there, including Somerville graduates like Muriel St Clare Byrne, Marjorie "Bar" Barber, Muriel "Jim" Jaeger, and also Eleanor Chase, a friend from Godolphin School days. Sayers also kept up with relations living in London. Dorothy Rowe was an easy train's journey away to the south-west in Bournemouth, where she had chosen to live and where she had found an outlet for her devotion to theatre. Doreen Wallace, however, an ex-Somerville writer like many of her friends, had found her place as a novelist and social campaigner (straining her friendship with the conservative Sayers) within the demands of farming and country life.[5] These educated women-friends all shared a similar challenge of finding their way in a changed world.

Sayers' first move was to seek some temporary school teaching, and also to fit in some ready translation work, until she found a permanent job which would support her work as a writer. Her experience teaching in Hull and her new Oxford MA would give her an easy doorway into school work, particularly giving French classes. In her temporary teaching jobs, she continued in her inimitable style. A pupil at the Girls' High School at Clapham vividly recalled that the teacher "grabbed a sword which was on the mantlepiece of the classroom and stumped up and down between the desks brandishing it above her head, quoting meantime from the *Pirates of Penzance* 'with-cat-like-tread-upon-our-prey-we-steal'".[6] Through this transitional and uncertain period, her parents were generously willing to give her what financial support they could, though she remained determined to become financially autonomous. Her desire to be a writer was clearly as strong as ever.

For almost a year she lived at 44, Mecklenburgh Square, an area of central London that was inhabited at often varying times by writers and artists, a number associated in some way with the Bloomsbury Group, and also the "other Bloomsbury" – that is, imagists poets and novelists like H.D. (Hilda Doolittle) and her husband Richard Aldington. D.H. Lawrence and his wife Frieda, who were connected with the imagists through Lawrence's poetry, had stayed very briefly in 44, Mecklenburgh

Square some time before Sayers moved into the same address. Sayers' fictional crime novelist, Harriet Vane, would live in the square at the time of her visit to her alma mater, "Shrewsbury College", in *Gaudy Night*. The opening of the novel describes Harriet sitting at a table by her window, where she often wrote. Instead of Harriet's eyes moving over her usual view of Mecklenburgh Square, they are drawn only to the letter before her, either one she has read or is writing. Whichever, the reader wonders: what is in the letter?[7]

At the end of 1921, with help from Muriel "Jim" Jaeger, Sayers moved nearby to 24, Great James Street, to just three white-panelled rooms – sitting-room, kitchen, and bedroom – with the use of a newly built bathroom and "lav". She was to lease these rooms and later additions for many years.

During the period living in Mecklenburgh Square, Sayers met one of the loves of her life, her passion far deeper than she had held for Whelpton, or than in her dramatic performances over Dr Hugh Allen at Oxford. John Cournos was a successful Jewish American writer, born in Kiev in the Ukraine twelve years before Sayers was born, and whose family emigrated to Philadelphia, USA, when he was ten.[8] Cournos fought his way out of poverty by going from office-boy to assistant editor at the *Philadelphia Record*. Though most of his earnings went to his family, he managed to make his way to London in 1912, there seeking freelance work and the woman he loved. As well as his journalism and book-writing, he became linked with the imagist movement through friendship with H.D. and Richard Aldington, and contributed to an early collection of imagist writing. He rented rooms on the floor above these friends living at 44, Mecklenburgh Square (before Sayers lived there), where the American woman he deeply loved and planned to marry, Dorothy Yorke, also stayed with the Aldingtons. Between serving in the First World War and on leave, Aldington entered into an affair with Yorke, which lasted long after the war, wounding Cournos. H.D., grieving over her stillborn child, and worried over the dangers her husband faced on the Western Front, tried to rationalize and accept the affair. In this state, she thought highly of Cournos, and later had a long, somewhat affectionate correspondence with him.[9]

Around that time it appeared that it was common for some characters in novels to be based in various degrees on actual people known to the author (such novels being labelled *roman à clef*). Under various names, Cournos appeared in novels by H.D. and others. In H.D.'s *Bid Me to Live* (1960) he would be portrayed as Ivan Levsky. He would also be recognizable as the murdered Philip Boyes in Sayers' *Strong Poison* (1930). Cournos was represented in Richard Aldington's *Death of a Hero* (1929), and with the name John Gombarov in his own trio of autobiographical novels (*The Mask, The Wall,* and *Babel,* 1919–22), and in *Miranda Masters* (1926, in which Miranda Masters is based on H.D.) as well as Richard Thorley in his *The Devil is an English Gentleman,* (1932), a revenge novel against Sayers. In her letters to Cournos, Sayers refers to lofty pronouncements in his writings as "J. Gombarov's sermons" and "J. Gombarov's philosophy", indicating her known reading of *The Mask* and *The Wall.* Her parents, at her suggestion, had also read *The Mask* and both liked it. Revd and Mrs Sayers were never to meet Cournos, despite Sayers' efforts, because of his reticence to visit them in Christchurch.

It is not clear how much Cournos confided in Sayers as their relationship deepened. The most we learn of their interaction is in bitter letters she wrote to Cournos after they went their separate ways at her request.[10] He may have told her of his experiences living for a time in Mecklenburgh Square with H.D. and Richard Aldington,[11] and meeting D.H. Lawrence and other imagists, as well as encountering at that time other writers who were associated with the Bloomsbury Group. Indeed, in his *Autobiography* (1935) Cournos mentions visiting Garsington Manor, near Oxford, where he wrote that Lady Ottoline Morrell "maintained a *salon*", where he records seeing W.B. Yeats, Lytton Strachey, Virginia Woolf, T.S. Eliot, and others.[12] As a poet herself, Sayers would have been interested in how the imagist movement construed the nature of images, and how they sought alternatives in modernism to the Victorian heritage, seeking a new foundation in the integrity of the image, and also in the ancient Near East and features of Hellenistic myth. Cournos himself had wide interests, revealed in the range of his publications, including many of his translations from Russian. Cournos and Sayers may well have touched on Judaism and Christianity. A writing shows his interest in Christianity, in his plea to fellow Jews in *Hear, O Israel*:

> ...Jesus stands as the very apex of Jewish
> culture. Can any Jew who has honestly studied
> the sayings and parables of Jesus deny this?
> And can he honestly reject him, exclude him
> from the hierarchy of Jewish prophets, of
> whom he is the logical culmination?
> ...Jews must remain Jews. Yet to remain Jews,
> they must take up their culture where they left
> off nineteen centuries ago. They must resume
> where they broke off the thread of their living
> tradition. They must challenge the world by
> affirming the best of their own culture – the
> culture of the Gospels. They must put forward
> the Struggle of the Jew Jesus as the only logical
> answer to *Mein Kampf*. The spirit of love and
> peace must be projected against the spirit of
> hatred and war. Only Contraries can meet

in battle: The Sermon on the Mount against
Brute Force.[13]

It is clear that Sayers had familiarity with recent writings such
as *The Mask* (1919) and probably knew of Cournos' extensive
edition, *The Best British Short Stories of 1922*, following his
omnibus pattern later in her three large volumes of stories of
detection and horror, but with much longer and more intensive
introductions than Cournos'.

Cournos had spent time in Devon during the war years
with H.D., Aldington, and other writers. There he had noticed
their expression of freedom which went far beyond free verse,
in their quest for the modern: the alternative to cultural and
social corsets and stiff clothing. In his later *Autobiography*
in 1935 (which left out Dorothy L. Sayers, but not Dorothy
Yorke), he records the group of writer friends beside the sea
throwing off their clothes and running into the water. Somehow
he was to persuade Sayers, who deeply appreciated the human
body that God has given, to lounge with him unclothed, when
she refused to consummate their relationship. Her Christian
convictions at that time made her see the desires of her body,
which she much appreciated, were only complete without the
interference of the "rubber-shop", and with the possibility of
a baby later appearing on the scene. She strongly wished for
marriage and children by him. Cournos, however, insisted that
he did not believe in marriage, and only wanted a full sexual
commitment to him, without possibility of children. In one of
her many letters to her mother, with whom she shared much,
Sayers rather sadly had to explain that she is unlikely to see
Cournos ever again. The reason was that they'd had a final
disagreement a few days before over Christian behaviour, to do
with an issue that he fiercely rejected. She does not reveal the
issue to her mother, but it was her refusal to agree to sexually

consummate her relationship with Cournos, involving the blocking of the possibility of conception.[14]

After Sayers had ended the relationship, John Cournos returned to America, leaving London in October 1922. In his *Autobiography*, he had said the five years following the end of the First World War "were mainly years of work, of friendship, of growing reputation as a writer, of interludes of living between books".[15] Back in the US, ironically, he soon married a New York writer of detective fiction under the name of Sybil Norton (real name Helen Satterthwaite), though, like Eric Whelpton before him, Cournos had had no time for what he openly thought a low-brow genre. His claim to be against marrying (he was certainly bruised by the abdication of his former fiancée, Dorothy Yorke), and avoiding having children, had proved to be deceptive, and many a time this unavoidable fact would leave Sayers secretly weeping. To add to her pain, Cournos' presumably hastily-found wife had two children from previous marriages.[16]

* * * * *

A child was born to Sayers on 3 January 1924, around fifteen months after the departure of John Cournos. He was called John[17] Anthony. The name of the father, William White, and his relationship with the mother, was carefully kept secret for many years, even from close friends, and also from Sayers' son himself. While on the rebound from Cournos, it was perhaps inevitable that Sayers would meet and be attracted to Bill White. He happened to be temporarily sharing a flat with friends on the floor above Sayers, in Great James Street.

Characteristically writing to her mother at Christchurch village, a few days before the Christmas of 1922, Sayers dramatically began her letter of Monday, 18 December by warning her mother not to faint from her message. She would be arriving home on Saturday. She would be travelling with a male friend on a motorbike. Her mother and father were about to discover the man was Bill White.[18] Unlike the elusive Cournos, Bill White had no qualms about visiting Sayers' parents with their daughter on the motorbike.

In his quest for ongoing work in the burgeoning motor trade, Bill had developed rather a nomadic existence. His wife and children often followed him around the country, but their base was always in Southbourne, Bournemouth, near where John Anthony was to be born. During their relationship, Bill omitted to tell Sayers that he was married, probably until after she revealed to him that she was pregnant. Bill's wife, totally opposite to the normal expectations, was remarkably kind to Sayers, helping her as much as she could. In fact, she invited Sayers to stay in Southbourne, near her, when the baby was due. She even arranged accommodation for her in a nearby guesthouse. Her patience with Bill delayed her divorce of him for several years. Sayers wasn't the first to fall under his charms. Though he had left a leading public school young, Bill retained what he had learned of Latin and Greek, and much else, and spoke fluent French (which would have particularly appealed to Sayers). For several years he had worked as a bank clerk in the City of London before joining the wartime army. His love of motors and motorcycles lead to his role in the First World War as a dispatch rider. He had even learned to fly while a clerk.

Sayers' pregnancy, which, given that she had capitulated to the benefits and failures of contraceptives, was unexpected, and immediately weighed down her plans to be a fully-fledged writer, earning her living for herself. She had already started a job she really loved at S.H. Benson, a leading advertising agency in London. It was largely unheard of for a new mother to keep on working, or, indeed, to find a means of keeping so. Pregnancy in the work place usually meant goodbye to the job. She undoubtedly was full of thought and concern about fostering the child growing in her. With her ability with making clothing and sewing she carefully created clothes to cover traces of her expanding body. Her main strategy was to exploit her hearty love of food. Her tall and slender build gradually grew into a most likely noticeable magnitude. She'd had to abandon her familiar body build for the sake of the work she loved, and for the prospect of self-reliance. Her keen-minded and witty colleagues at the agency didn't seem to notice the gradual transformation. By then, her second Peter Wimsey novel was in process, and the company, who had a number of graduates in their employ, responded to her request for some time off to finish it. This allowed her to return to work some time after the early January birth of John Anthony.[19]

The pressure and dilemmas of the decisions Sayers had had to make over the forthcoming birth can be seen in how she left it to almost the last minute to ask her older cousin Ivy Shrimpton if she would foster John Anthony, and to keep hidden from her parents and friends who the mother of Ivy's latest foster child was. Even though the father, Bill White, had abruptly broken away from his flirtations with Sayers upon hearing of the pregnancy, the end of 1923 had found Sayers in Southbourne. Was it possible that Sayers had a faint hope that Bill's wife, living nearby, might take on the child? Then just two days before the birth, she took the risk of asking Ivy about fostering the baby. She knew her cousin well, and her work with her mother, Sayer's aunt Amy Shrimpton, in fostering children. At first Sayers only wrote of a baby about to be born that needed foster care but a few weeks after confessing it was hers, she took John Anthony to Ivy's then home in 45, Oxford Road, Cowley, on the southern edge of Oxford.

In her unfinished novel based on her own life, *Cat o'
Mary*, Sayers revealed her deeper feelings about giving birth to
a child, separately from all the issues arising from her infant's
illegitimacy. This was the Sayers who had longed to have babies
with Cournos, the lover from whom she'd had to break free.[20]
Just like other women, she was going to have a baby. The body
she had been given, would be serving her in a very good way.

* * * * *

Later that year, in autumn 1924, and then throughout 1925,
Sayers took up a correspondence with Cournos. Quite
understandably, it focused largely on his treachery. To be fair,
however, she actually had benefitted from their friendship. In
terms of her demanding commitment to achieve a writing life,
Cournos had provided a godsend to a fledgling author of stories
of detection. Not only would she have gained insights from the
wide variety of his high productivity, but he introduced her to
his literary agent, Andrew Dakers, who took her on. Dakers was
able to place the first "Peter Wimsey", as Sayers called it, with
Cournos' publisher in New York – Boni and Liveright. *Whose
Body?* was published in 1923, followed by a British edition later
that year with T. Fisher Unwin.

There are ambiguities, however, in Sayers' often bitter letters
to John Cournos where, when he was on a visit to London, she
invited him several times to drop by. The tone of the letters also
changes at the very end of the correspondence, according to
her biographer and goddaughter, Barbara Reynolds – probably
because she had now met another man, named "Mac", whom
she was eventually to marry. Cournos had sent her a copy of
an article written by G.K. Chesterton, on "How to Write a
Detective Story", in case she hadn't seen it. In the letter she
responds warmly to receiving it, thanking Cournos for saving

her six pennies, as she had planned to buy the issue of *G.K.'s Weekly* which carried it (on 17 October 1925). She applauded the article as one of the best and most serviceable examples of an item of analysis she had come across for a long period.

"Mac" was the nickname of the man Sayers had met, and would soon marry, and who allowed her to leave behind her grief over Cournos and over the dashing father of John Anthony, though she still kept her liking for motor vehicles, and particularly motorbikes. "Mac" was Oswald Atherton Fleming.[21] Fleming shared Sayers' interest in motoring, photography, crime writing, and good food, and was a dab hand at cookery. He also painted and illustrated. He was by then a seasoned Fleet Street journalist, working for *News of the World* as motoring and crime correspondent, and writer of books; he had panache and Sayers enjoyed his buoyant company. He was a natural storyteller. A later book of Mac's *The Gourmet's Book of Food and Drink*, was dedicated to his wife "who can make an omelette".[22]

In her later follow-up novel, *Strong Poison* (1930), which indirectly points darkly toward Cournos, Sayers introduces crime writer Harriet Vane and with her a strong love interest into Wimsey's life. It is followed by *Have His Carcase* (1932). In the opening of this novel, Sayers writes with feeling about Harriet's bruised heart. She had not accepted Wimsey's love for her as the remedy for her ills. Instead, she had before her three things that she felt were much more effective for healing: her authentic work, her physical activities (such as the coastal walking-tour she had just started), and a recent abundance of wealth following from her acquittal for murder as a well-known crime writer.

Atherton Fleming was not to provide wealth, but he did encourage her passionate work, and indeed made work even more necessary as his health gradually sapped and the upkeep of young John Anthony by Ivy Shrimpton and later, schooling, increased in cost as Sayers' child grew.

Fleming was over eleven years older than Sayers, and was born in Orkney in 1881 (hence "Mac"), with the family soon moving to northern England. By the time of the unknown date he met her, perhaps in 1925, he'd had a varied life. He had married Winifred Meyrick (a daughter, like Sayers, of the manse) in 1911, and became the father of two daughters. During the Boer war he had been a newspaper correspondent, and in the First World War, he became a war correspondent for the *Daily Chronicle* and *The Sunday Chronicle*, but became badly affected by being wounded and gassed. On his return to civilian life he often substituted his proper rank of Captain for the more impressive fake title of "Major". He authored – probably with the vast number of those bereaved in mind – a popular guide to places where so many had died in the First World War: *How to See the Battlefields*. This included insights into the realities of the conflict from his own experience in the Royal Army Service Corps. He wrote of

> ...the poor devils who – many times – worked
> forty-eight hours on end, at least half of the
> time under shell-fire, plunging and wallowing
> in and out of shell-holes, lorries heavily laden
> with shells and cartridges, well over the axles
> in mud, no lights, and very often no food,
> and not the slightest protection in the way of
> trench or dug-out when the road was under
> fire.... And yet, in spite of it all, the guns
> were fed and the shells arrived at the batteries
> somehow or other! When looking at these
> roads and tracks in the Somme area – roads up
> to the battery positions – try to imagine what
> it must have been like to work without lights
> at night – battery positions cannot be reached

in the daytime except on certain occasions
– and when the least error of judgment or
sleepiness on the part of the drivers might
precipitate both lorry and contents into some
huge shell-hole or mine crater.[23]

Gradually, the effects of Mac's wartime experiences were to become more and more evident in what much later would be labelled as "post-traumatic stress disorder", experiences which were to have a debilitating effect on their marriage. Eventually he was no longer able to work. In Sayers' first Lord Peter Wimsey novel, *Whose Body* (1923), written before she knew Mac, Wimsey, the private detective, had vividly showed searing signs of emotional wounding from his wartime experience. The literary type of the damaged detective is still alive and well, as displayed in war-wounded Cormoran Strike in J.K. Rowling's popular crime novels (2013–20), Rowling writing as Robert Galbraith.

Because of the Christian beliefs that Sayers held and which had survived through difficult years, she thought much about the reality of sin in her moral struggles. She knew that her faith was not founded upon deep spiritual emotion, but was related to the reality of human sin in a fallen and disrupted world, which she had by necessity to think through with what she was to call the "passionate intellect". She had, in particular, to wrestle with her sexuality and the strong and very real natural demands of her body. Cournos' indifference to the roots of her resistance to a sexual consummation without the natural consequences, grieved her. When she gave in to Bill White, not knowing he was married, she still then had to search her heart regarding her own responsibility in that relationship. If she had later discovered that Mac's adultery some years before had precipitated his very recent divorce, in May 1925, she would have been strong enough, it seems, from her own wrestling over sin to accept him. Even if she did not know the cause of his divorce, she was nevertheless able to continue to accept and love him when he brought many difficulties into their married life. No doubt, because of her self-knowledge over sin, a state she took with great seriousness, she also was in all likelihood aware of how difficult she could be. She was no Pharisee.

As Mac had been divorced, there was no possibility of a church wedding at those times, so the only option was for their wedding to take place in a registry office. The place they chose for the marriage on 13 April 1926 was in Clerkenwell Road, London, not far from Sayers' flat in Great James Street. Sayers took "Fleming" for her married name, keeping her maiden name for "books and business". At the Christchurch rectory, Helen Sayers, with Henry, drank a parental glass of champagne on the day. The newlyweds celebrated afterwards, drinking considerably more than her parents, along with many of Mac's Fleet Street friends at the Falstaff pub, apparently a haven for journalists.[24] Sayers had contemplated renting a larger flat to accommodate the two of them after marriage. She had also turned over in her mind the possibility of taking in John Anthony, but the fact that both of them were working made this still unfeasible. However, the two were to settle at number 24, and later took on more rooms from the floor above (presumably where Bill White had once stayed with friends), to expand their living area effectively into a maisonette.

When Sayers was informing Ivy Shrimpton about her marriage to Mac, and its implications for the care of John Anthony, she made it clear that she wished for Ivy to carry on caring for the child. She said she would soon come down to see Ivy in Oxford so that they could talk things through. This would also give chance for Mac to meet both Ivy and John Anthony. She pointed out in the same letter that Mac seemed happy to take responsibility over John Anthony in the future.[25] Ivy in fact was the first Sayers told of her imminent wedding, having John Anthony in the forefront of her concerns.

When Mac piled his things into Sayers' few rooms at 24, Great James Street, it emphasized the smallness of what was to be their joint accommodation. Nevertheless they settled into the cramped flat and made the best of it for the time being. It had a strong advantage of being midway between the advertising agency where Sayers worked, and the newspaper world of Fleet Street.

Following Sayers' revelation to Ivy about the wedding, she now had no option but to rather abruptly inform her parents, whom she knew would have dreamed of a church wedding for the daughter they loved and cherished. She did this in a racy letter to her mother on 8 April, only five days before the wedding, thus making sure that there was no time to inform the wider family and give time for preparation to be at the ceremony. As well as giving the unexpected news of the sudden wedding, Sayers also chose to briefly introduce Mac in the letter's brief compass. As always her father, and her mother who was so close to her, stood by their daughter's wishes. Henry Sayers immediately sent a cheque, and Helen Sayers wrote a very positive letter. Sayers assured her mother that she and Mac would come to Christchurch at Whitsun to see them. In answer to a question about what she would wear from her mother, Sayers wrote back that she would be married in green.

The new Mrs Fleming and Mac made their way to Christchurch through the flat Fen country for a three-day stay with her parents during Whitsun, with Whit Sunday falling on 23 May that year. The couple arrived on Sayers' Ner-A-Car, which was a popular motorcycle and sidecar combination at that time. During the visit, Sayers' mother characteristically took up a sporting chance to be driven by her daughter. She thoroughly enjoyed being driven at speed sitting in the sidecar for a short run, Sayers told Ivy Shrimpton in a letter just after the visit. It then was Ivy's turn to receive the two of them at her Cowley home, the following Thursday. The weather had turned very wet, and Sayers had warned Ivy humorously that Mac didn't like riding in the open sidecar in the rain. Ivy therefore would not have been surprised to meet the motorcyclist and her passenger in that unusual arrangement. She was used to the unexpected ways of her cousin, with whom she had much in common, and in all likelihood very much enjoyed them, given her open acceptance of Sayers.

John Anthony at that time was in his third year, and knew his mother simply as "Cousin Dorothy", and Mac was to become "Cousin Mac". The visit went well, and presumably the young child's future was discussed, with Sayers maybe speaking about her wish for him to go at the right age to a good school like Malvern College in Worcestershire, a boarding school that thirteen years before C.S. Lewis (then unknown to Sayers) had reluctantly attended. When the two eventually set off for London, they went in the direction of Henley, passing Dorchester-on-Thames, Wallingford, and the slowly winding Thames, stopping off in Henley on an important mission. Mac the gourmet had arranged to pick up a large cooked ham from a food expert he knew in the town. At that point, Sayers took on the role of carrying the ham carefully, sitting clasping it in the sidecar, as they proceeded back to London. Mac and Sayers often had disagreements as to who should ride the motorbike and who should be seated in the sidecar. Eventually, at Mac's insistence, they bought a small car, a Belsize-Bradshaw coupé, and sold the Ner-A-Car. Sayers however kept for her use a previous motorcycle, which she had before buying the Ner-A-Car in order to convey the both of them, and hadn't parted with. This was a solo two-stroke bike. Sayers clearly preferred motorbikes to cars, unless they were the cars liked by Lord Peter Wimsey in her detective stories.

In February that year, Sayers' second Peter Wimsey, *Clouds of Witness*, had been published, and a third was well advanced. As Sayers was gradually becoming known to the public, it was therefore not only her marriage, modes of transport, the shortage of space at Great James Street, and the demands of her job, that were on her mind. Sayers and Mac decided to let it be publicly known that they were adopting John Anthony, which didn't affect their arrangement with Ivy. Later the child's surname was established as "Fleming". However, they never did bring John Anthony into their household to be his home. The secret of her son out of wedlock was never publicly revealed during Sayers' lifetime, and only was to be discovered some years after her death by her first biographer, Janet Hitchman.[26]

Ivy, with her mother Amy, continued therefore to be a huge support to her in fostering John Anthony, because of her thoughtfulness. No doubt the fact that Ivy was part of Sayers' extended family, a cousin with whom she'd had a rapport since her early childhood, was significant. Ivy notably was also within the Leigh side of the family. Sayers (Dorothy *Leigh* Sayers) had an open affinity with the Leighs through her closeness to her mother, and through her Aunt Amy Shrimpton (her mother's widowed sister), her widowed Aunt Maud (who had married Henry Leigh, her mother's brother), Maud's daughter – her cousin the writer Margaret Leigh – and others. Through Ivy, Sayers was therefore able to continue working after her marriage to Mac, gradually supporting him more and more in his slow decline.

6

GUINNESS WAS GOOD FOR HER
(1922–29)

The Novel and the Play are twin-sisters in the
family of fiction...
**Wilkie Collins, Letter of Dedication to
Charles James Ward, Esq**[1]

S.H. Benson was one of the largest and most successful
advertising and publicity agencies in Britain in the 1920s,
eventually to take on the creation of innovative Guinness
adverts as part of its varied range, many of which would become
legendary.[2] Sayers, soon after settling in London and possessing
her newly received Oxford University degrees of BA honours
and MA, applied to work at the agency as an " ideas man" and
copywriter. Its offices at Kingsway near central London were
close to where she lived – just ten minutes' walk. In doing
so she was turning away from her chances of school teaching
and even university teaching, which most likely would have
welcomed her outstanding intellectual talents. She was still
gambling upon making authorship her chosen work, with her
earnings from copywriting in advertising making this possible.
Her time at Benson's, however, was to mean much more than
gaining a supportive income through good work well done.

Long later, the writer of her obituary in *The Times,* who clearly understood her, wrote about her trying her hand in the world of advertising: "The directness and the grasp of facts that are needed by a copywriter stood her in good stead as a newcomer to the crowded ranks of authors of detective fiction."[3] Sayers indeed admired the copywriter, and is quoted as saying that their grasp of English is "the richest, noblest, most flexible and sensitive language ever written or spoken".[4]

Her preliminary weekly salary at Benson's was better than she could attain in school teaching. When the post was confirmed after a trial period, in the early summer of 1922 she reported to her parents that she had been informed that she possessed the necessary and unique traits of a successful person in advertising.[5] Some weeks later she made a sumptuous five-course meal for John Cournos by way of celebration. She could give him a delightful meal but, being wary, she could not offer him her inexperienced body in free love, in the light of her convictions. She was further pleased when Benson's very soon increased her weekly wage from £4 to £5.

Following the departure of Cournos back to the US, and after Sayers had encountered Bill White, the lift in her spirit had become obvious in inviting White as her guest to one of the dances held at Benson's. Her new mood was perhaps echoed in the rise of the Jazz age. Perhaps surprisingly she even played a saxophone for a staff dance. She had in the past been seriously absorbed by the piano and violin, so it was a dramatic move.[6]

Sayers' love of company fitted well with working in a creative climate of advertising. Though she was generating ideas that would have popular appeal, and copywriting, she was also working with graphic designers to whom she could present visual ideas as well as words, bringing together playful and attractively compact results. Together they could share the enjoyment of hitting a successful message. Sayers was undoubtedly talented visually as well as verbally. Not only could she create text, but also pattern it and integrate illustrations into it, her sketches of which designers could enhance and complete. Over the years this would be demonstrated in the varied and notable advertising campaigns that she was involved in, such as Guinness beer campaigns, and that of Norwich's Colman's Mustard, which became an enduring hit with the public through the inspired creation of the Mustard Club, which adorned billboard and the sides of buses – adverts which carried a continuing story or theme.[7]

Sayers was heavily involved with both campaigns from the beginning. It is likely that her hand was in the names given to the members of the Mustard Club, who became household names, due to the success of the advertising. These included the club's officers, Lord Bacon of Cookham, the president Baron de Beef, and the club's secretary, a Miss Di Gester. Membership rules for the club were created, one of which was: "Every member shall see that the mustard is freshly made, and no member shall tip a waiter who forgets to put mustard on the table."

Also produced for the Mustard Club was a popular recipe book. Sayers drew Mac , with his culinary knowledge, heavily into the creation of its recipes. Under the impetus of its advertising drives, the Mustard Club was featured throughout newspapers and magazines, often in cartoon form. Its message of mustard improving health and easing the blight of indigestion got onto dining tables everywhere.

Benson's Guinness campaign began in 1928, which drew in the combined skills of Sayers and the painter and illustrator John Gilroy (later the much sought-after Sir John Gilroy). Five years younger than her, Gilroy had joined Benson's in 1925, and was soon involved in the Mustard Club campaigns. It was convenient that Sayers' office was at the top of the spiral staircase, and Gilroy's at the bottom; this found her often running up and down it during the high-paced work on the Guinness advertisements. In later years Gilroy was to become famous for his portraits of great figures in the theatre, politics, among royalty, and others. His subjects were to include Lord Mountbatten and the Queen and, while he was at Benson's, he painted and drew a still youthful Sayers, whom he was much taken with. He appreciated, with his artist's eyes, her "terrific size – lovely fat fingers – lovely snub nose – lovely curly lips – a baby's face in a way."[8] More effectively than these words, his portrait and drawing of her capture her personality and appearance very strongly and engagingly. In her portrait she is smiling, a subtle smile, and wearing a white wig that does not distract. It was a wig that would help her at times when her hair would become very thin, an affliction she bore stoically and buoyantly. The portrait was made in the year Sayers, in her late thirties, was finally able to leave Benson's. The drawing was sketched in the next year, and both reveal the trust and appreciation she had in Gilroy's work.[9] In his biography of Sayers, James Brabazon points out that the painting and drawings of Sayers captured her at the threshold of her well-known presence as crime writer, BBC Radio broadcaster, and dramatist.[10]

Sayers and Gilroy helped to create together the famous "Zoo" theme in Guinness advertising. Among her advertising copy was the famous Toucan verse which proclaimed the goodness of Guinness.

The jingle was enhanced by Gilroy's distinctive cartoon of a happy toucan with its exaggerated bill over two pint glasses of Guinness stout. The Gilroy Zoo contained other animals as the name suggests, as well as the toucan, including sea-lions, elephants, lions, bears, gnus, pelicans, and ostriches. For half a century, the toucan remained part of the brewer's corporate image.[11] Gilroy caricatured himself as a cartoon zookeeper.

As well as her powerful advertising copy, Sayers' visual imagination was constantly at play, resulting in rough sketches which Gilroy adapted and enhanced into his memorable illustrations. The two clearly enjoyed creating together, an effective duo somewhat like, in a different mode and behind the scenes, Laurel and Hardy in cinema and Gilbert and Sullivan on the stage, but whose advertising output was widely popular.

In later years, famous among other work for his portraits, the artist said that Sayers had become one of the memorable figures in his life.

* * * * *

During their busy weeks and months Sayers and Mac were still able to take a number of holidays, though they often took work with them. Some of the breaks provided settings for her detective stories: the Galloway and Dumfries area in southern Scotland would one day provide a rich landscape for her *Five Red Herrings* (*Suspicious Characters* in the US). In the early summer of 1926, not long after their marriage, Sayers and Mac had taken a holiday in the New Forest in Hampshire, an area of open heath and woodland, where in general the land is mildly undulating. The New Forest was chosen as the Ner-A-Car was not good at climbing steeper slopes, especially with the two of them weighing it down. Sayers often said that she loved the city and hated the countryside. But, in fact, in some of her detective novels, she writes vividly and observantly of the countryside, though often intermittently. For instance, in *Clouds of Witness* she writes of Lord Peter in the Yorkshire Moors making his way to a farmhouse, neighbouring his brother's large country house, at one stage squelching his way downhill following a sheep-path. In describing the New Forest holiday to her mother in a letter she praised the woodland in brief postcard style, only noting how beautiful the forest was, and that the weather was mostly good But at that point in the letter her memories are taken over by her disappointment that Mac's upset stomach was unrelenting, making him miserable the whole time during the holiday. She put his discomfort down to the continued effects of being gassed in the First World War. She was aware of his talents in a number of areas, including his journalism, and how the discomforts that physically blighted him affected his work, and, relatedly, his temper.[12]

* * * * *

Sayers was to serve nearly eight years at Benson's, and her time there was full of vivid memories. Soon after leaving she began a new Sir Peter Wimsey adventure based around a company called Pym's Advertising Agency, closely modelled upon Benson's. *Murder Must Advertise* brings to life its long corridors with glass-panelled office doors either side. An iron spiral staircase connects the floors, as in Benson's Kingsway Hall, and plays an important part in the murder unveiled in the story. Some characters in the novel are based upon Benson staff familiar to Sayers. One young woman, Miss Meteyard, dressed in Sayers' favourite green, is even based on the author herself. In one place, Mr Ingleby, one of the management, says Miss Meteyard was educated at Somerville College. He added that she is among the brightest in the advertising department, and capable of creating the crudest limericks. Mr Ingleby himself is based upon the distinguished Robert "Bobby" A. Bevan, who joined Benson's the year after Sayers.[13] As the novel opens, the reader is taken immediately into the corridors and offices of Pym's Agency, and introduced to several characters, including Miss Meteyard and a new copywriter who replaces a staff member recently killed in a fall down the stairway. The new copywriter, called Mr Death Bredon ("Death" pronounced *Deeth*), is in fact Lord Peter Wimsey in disguise, intent on secretly investigating what he suspects is a murder, not an accident, and uncovers much more going on in the advertising agency, unknown to its largely innocent staff.

Sayers' first biographer, Janet Hitchman, observes:

> The characters in *Murder Must Advertise* are a mixture of her fellow staff. She jumbled up a trait of this one, with the looks of that, but several of them are quite recognizable. The head of her department, Mr. Oswald Greene, came out as Mr. Armstrong, and Mr. Jayne, another copy director, as Mr. Hankin. She wrote herself in as Miss Meteyard, the plain, Oxford educated copywriter, never at a loss for an apt quotation.[14]

Not only does the novel take us fictionally into the active world of the Benson company, but also into London in the 1920s, including its pubs, the bright and creative university graduates which made up a number of Benson's staff members, and the street drugs trade which would not stop at murder or infiltrating what the seasoned Mr Ingleby says is an old-fashioned firm. In the author's note at the beginning of the novel, Sayers takes pains to state, slightly tongue in the cheek, perhaps, that advertising people are strict law abiders and altogether harmless, and so for any murder to be committed on their premises, it could only be the idea of a crime writer looking to make guilty the most unlikely person.

Though Sayers relished working in advertising, and at Benson's in particular, she does point out in her novel the social damage caused by the increase of advertising in her day. She has

Lord Peter saying it is like having yeast in bread. As often, his speaking echoes the Authorized Version of the Bible, on which he had been brought up, though not in fact a Christian believer, nor critical of Christian belief. Wimsey proclaims, drawing on a biblical parable, that any truth to be found in adverts is like the leaven hidden by a woman in ground-up grain, creating enough of a gas blast to cause a misshapen form digestible to the public.

In later years, when Sayers had established herself publicly as an essayist and commentator on modern society – particularly in the climate of war, and the threat and damage of war – she was to speak up controversially about the harmful effects of advertising in the context of contemporary education. This was in her famous "The Lost Tools of Learning" lecture in 1947, which was published as a pamphlet in 1948.[15]

She continued to find herself relishing and thankful for the work she threw herself into at Benson's, not least in its making her writing possible (she published four of her Wimsey books while there), and also providing the income to support the care given to John Anthony by her cousin Ivy. Not long after her marriage to Mac, however, there was a crisis she had to face with the sudden death of Ivy's mother, Sayers' Aunt Amy. Amy Shrimpton had played a vital role in the fostering of John Anthony and others, including a child called Isobel Tovey, a little older than Sayers' son. Though Ivy was a trustworthy carer, she'd had no formal training in fostering. The sudden loss of Amy meant, it seemed, that Ivy would need to find a job, which would be very difficult without training, and working for someone else would mean that Ivy would not be able to carry on fostering John Anthony. If Sayers and Mac had to take in John Anthony, on the other hand, it would jeopardize their work, especially as Mac's slowly developing handicaps meant that Sayers was gradually earning what would become their entire income. It was a dilemma for both Ivy and Sayers, who empathized with each other. It would also mean Ivy moving from Cowley in order to cover the costs and so as to continue caring for John Anthony. In moving, Ivy would need to find a desirable country cottage to rent, and this played on her mind.

In order to help Ivy after the death of Amy, Helen Sayers paid her a visit and was able to talk over the possibilities with Ivy. A poignancy was that Helen saw her grandson for the very first time, but without it being unveiled to her that she was in fact John Anthony's grandmother. Sayers had had to work through whether or not to inform her. But knowing that Helen had now seen John Anthony wasn't enough to convince her that it was time to tell her mother, to whom she was so close, the true story of the infant. Her parents were to go to their shared grave unaware they were grandparents. They had not had the chance to be more involved in helping their daughter to resolve her difficulties, or even to understand them.

As Ivy, Sayers, and Mac chewed over the difficult issues, Ivy found a possible cottage to rent, which would be suitable for caring for just John Anthony and Isobel. It was in the small village of Westcott Barton, in Oxfordshire, near Chipping Norton, and fairly near Banbury. Like many houses in the Cotswold hills, "The Sidlings"[16] was built with local sand-coloured stones. It was old, dating back to 1727, with a tall roof and lacking an indoor water supply; water was retrieved from a tap near the back entrance. Today, the thatched roof of Ivy's time has been replaced by slate roofing. Ivy, who'd had a tough upbringing, decided that this was the place where she could afford to continue caring for her two charges. Sayers and Mac had discussed the possibility of moving to Banbury (maybe because it was nearer to John Anthony), and commuting to London, which would be very difficult, given that Sayers had to be at Kingsway Hall by 9:30 am on Mondays. Discussion about Banbury was just part of Mac's quest to find a country cottage for Sayers and himself, from which they could commute to London. The idea was to retain the flat at 24, Great James Street for living in during the working week.

Some of the tensions of living in the small spaces of the flat were relieved by being able to add the number of rooms on the extra floor that had become free to rent. According to Sayers' authorized biographer, James Brabazon, both Mac and Sayers were people who needed space in their home, and lack of it could raise tensions. However, even with the extra space at Great James Street, Mac's idea of having a country cottage had appeal. Both of them were working hard, even though Mac was now only able to be working just around half of the time. With him continuing to report on cuisine, motor sports, and crime, while Sayers was writing her succession of detective stories as well as creating imaginative ads for Benson's, the quest for a country cottage wasn't a priority. But Mac continued to be preoccupied with the idea. With the crisis of John Anthony's care resolved, there was however another blow about to bring grief to the couple.

On 20 September 1928, when Sayers and Mac were working away at the London flat organizing and decorating, along with the necessary workmen – including plumbers, electricians, and gas-fitters – who were adding on the rooms in the floor above, Sayers had an unexpected telephone message, via the village post office, from the rectory in Christchurch. Her father had just died from pneumonia. In a letter informing Ivy of her uncle's death, and how it would not affect their finances in continuing to pay for her care of John Anthony, Sayers added that, mercifully, he had suddenly passed away in peace. Benson's gave Sayers leave of absence, and she went ahead of Mac to Christchurch. As she travelled there to help her mother with the after effects of Henry's death, she no doubt was turning over in her mind the dilemma of housing her mother. With the rector dead, the house would be needed for a replacement incumbent.

Mac worked quickly, already having conducted a fair amount of research on possible places outside of London where he and Sayers could buy a weekend country cottage. No doubt his focus would have been on places with accessible train routes out of London. The death of Henry Sayers reorientated everything. Mac found a house for sale on a rail link northeast out of London. Sunnyside Cottage, on Newland Street (the main street), at number 24, was for sale in Witham, Essex. This was now seen as a house that Helen Sayers might live in, rather than creating a weekend dwelling for Mac and Sayers. On 18 October, less than a month after Henry's death, Sayers wrote to Ivy that they had purchased a home that clearly from her description was just right for them: it was pretty with being Georgian, and with garden and courtyard, and other good features she listed.

It was necessary to bring in decorators before her mother could move in. Mac took his mother-in-law to the house to choose wallpapers and other things. He had reported to Sayers afterwards that she wasn't able to "see anything but gloom and difficulties", which had a depressing effect on him, who was suffering badly from nerves. Sayers wrote to Ivy about her mother's visit and how busy the last month had been, and that the pace would continue right up to Christmas. It would include the house move, with Aunt Mabel joining her in Witham. Mabel Leigh was Helen Sayers' sister, who had lived at the rectory in Christchurch, and before that in Bluntisham. The rather gloomy mood of the letter continues with Sayers observing that her mother complained that Henry Sayers, for the last forty years or so, had really been no companion to her, but now she missed him terribly. She closes the letter by asking Ivy to forgive her somewhat moaning letter. Sayers in fact was quite positive over the move and all it entailed; she regarded being able to find and buy Sunnyside in Witham rather miraculous. She had never actually warmed to Christchurch, unlike Bluntisham. She had once even joked to Eric Whelpton that Christchurch was the final place God put there, and after finishing he noticed he had omitted a staircase!

Sayers' income at this time was steadily rising, what with her book sales and her healthy income from Benson's, but the addition of money from her mother, and a legacy from Sayers' Uncle Percy Leigh, who had died in Australia, was opportune for buying Sunnyside. She would eventually be able to buy number 22, Chantry Cottage, the house next door, when it became available, and connect the two houses into one, providing much more space. In the distant past numbers 22, 24, and 26 had once in fact been one extensive tenement along Newland Street, historically with the name "Cocksmiths", which at one time was the name of number 26. Timbers in the building date back to the fifteenth century, and frontages of grey-brick were placed during the nineteenth century. The "Cocksmiths" properties, sometimes called "Dorothy Sayers Cottages", are now Grade-II listed.[17]

Helen Sayers' perception of the house grew more positive after she and Aunt Mabel moved in, and Mac and Sayers were able to stay with them in Sunnyside over Christmas. As winter passed, spring came, and summer began to wane, her mother settled fully into her new life, shared with her elderly sister.

But her mother died suddenly on 27 July 1929 as a result of a rupture of her bowel, which led to a stoppage. She had refused to have a doctor summoned, or for her daughter to be called from London. By the time Mac and Sayers were called, it was too late. It was an enormous shock for Sayers, who had been so close to her mother. In a letter to Ivy giving details of her mother's death she confessed that she found it hard to accept that her mother had gone; it seemed like she was still there in what had become her home.

Ivy had offered to come to Witham to help with caring for Aunt Mabel, an offer Sayers appreciated, but she explained in the same letter that she and Mac would be living there for weekends right up to when she would leave Benson's at the end of the year. After that, their move to Witham would be essentially permanent. They would continue to use their flat at Great James Street when necessary. It was very convenient, she felt, that Witham was so close to the city that they could with no trouble get to and fro. She also revealed her thinking about her son, John Anthony, that the house would be his home one day. She carefully qualified this by adding that it was unlikely her Aunt Mabel would be able to cope with children around the house, even though she was bearing her long years well.

Her mother's death had probably precipitated Sayers' decision over when to leave Benson's. Mac's work was clearly slowing down even more, and her publishers in the US had made a significant agreement with her which made it unnecessary for her to continue with the "office work" at the advertising agency. Though she knew she would greatly miss the social aspect of Benson's and its camaraderie, and the play of creating compact jingles, slogans, sketches, and witticisms, her work was about to enter another chapter. It would involve the serious business of death, and the taking of a literary oath over a human skull.

7

LORD PETER WIMSEY AND ERIC THE SKULL: WITHIN THE GOLDEN AGE OF THE DETECTION CLUB (1930–36)

> 'Here I am about to die, but you know that I
> am innocent, that these men are lying. Why
> must I die?'
>
> **Susanna 1:43, *Good News Bible, Catholic
> edition***[1]

In 1920 or so, when fresh from France, Sayers had been struck with the idea of creating what were increasingly popular detective stories for the welcome reward of money. When writing her introduction to an omnibus of connected short stories, relating to detection, horror, and mystery, around ten years later, she remembered an event from her first settling in London.

As she reflected back a decade or more her vivid memory was of a friend and herself on a rainy Sunday, wondering what to do that day. They decided to make their way to one of the large central railway stations. There they knew would be a large bookstall almost certainly laden with popular novels. Though it was a faint hope at that period, they thought they might possibly come across a crime story to read aloud to each other.

Good fortune was with them. They happened upon *Through the Wall* (1909), a significant crime mystery of its time, by American author Cleveland Moffett, and set in France. Sayers considered that, ten years on, the two of them would certainly expect to have to decide between maybe twenty novels of detection, all written skilfully and brought out by excellent publishers.

The two friends understandably praised each other for their find, and were soon into the first chapter of Cleveland Moffett, which began:

> It is worthy of note that the most remarkable
> criminal case in which the famous French
> detective, Paul Coquenil, was ever engaged, a
> case of more baffling mystery than the Palais
> Royal diamond robbery and of far greater
> peril to him than the Marseilles trunk drama
> – in short, a case that ranks with the most
> important ones of modern police history
> – would never have been undertaken by
> Coquenil (and in that event might never have
> been solved) but for the extraordinary faith
> this man had in certain strange intuitions or
> forms of half knowledge that came to him at
> critical moments of his life, bringing marvelous
> guidance.[2]

Lord Peter Wimsey had been created way back in 1920, when the seeds of what became Sayers' first murder mystery, *Whose Body?*, were emerging. When the manuscript was eventually completed, and ready for typing up, she was already weary of him, or even appalled by him, and complained so to her mother! Agatha Christie, who like Sayers was at the centre of the Golden Age of detection fiction, would one day advise budding crime writers, "Be very careful what central character you create – you may have him with you for a very long time!"[3]

Sayers had worked hard on that first Wimsey manuscript during August and September of 1921 while staying at her parents' home in Christchurch. The character of Lord Peter would quite quickly develop and become more rounded as other Wimsey books followed. Essentially, she was discovering in writing the novels that characters in the stories had to be allowed to have a life of their own. She would also eventually discover that when a love interest finds its way into the plot, it served to add to the lovers involved more of the very mystery of a human being, even though fictional. In so doing, she was to reject her strong view that it was a bad idea to introduce a love interest into detective stories, as this weakened, she had thought, the strong rational and orderly structure of such stories.

Many years later C.S. Lewis, who would get to know Sayers well as a friend, wrote a celebratory piece for her funeral, which had to be read out for him in his reluctant absence:

> I have heard it said that Lord Peter is the only
> imaginary detective who ever grew up – grew
> from the Duke's son, the fabulous amorist,
> the scholar swashbuckler, and connoisseur of
> wine, into the increasingly human character,
> not without quirks and flaws, who loves
> and marries, and is nursed by, Harriet Vane.
> Reviewers complained that Miss Sayers was
> falling in love with her hero. On which a better
> critic remarked to me, "It would be truer to
> say she was falling out of love with him; and
> ceased fondling a girl's dream – if she had ever
> done so – and began inventing a man." There

is in reality no cleavage between the detective
stories and her other works. In them, as in it,
she is first and foremost the craftsman, the
professional. She always saw herself as one
who has learned a trade, and respects it, and
demands respect for it from others.[4]

By the time of the house move to Witham that took place about
eight years later, in 1929, as many as five Wimsey books had
been published, and another was in preparation.[5] In that year
of the move Sayers had had to say farewell to her colleagues
at Benson's, but she had by then also joined a new group of
like-minded people in London which was to mean much to
her – a group which was to expand and eventually be called
the "Detection Club". Important also to her was that she met
the Australian novelist Helen de Guerry Simpson through the
club, who had been in Oxford when Sayers was studying at
Somerville College, though their paths didn't cross at that time.
The highly talented Helen Simpson however, four years younger
than Sayers, had been drawn into the club's circle. She was to
become an important friend who shared her Christian faith.[6]
The club had started to take shape in 1928 and 1929, even
though it is now usually said that it was established in 1930,
which is when it was formalized and its first president, G.K.
Chesterton took office. Chesterton of course was the famous
author of stories of the clerical amateur detective Father Brown,
and of wildly imaginative but powerfully ordered novels such
as *The Man Who Was Thursday* and *The Napoleon of Notting Hill*.
Sayers had heard him speak on a couple of occasions when she
was an undergraduate at Somerville, and owed him a debt for
developing and even recovering her Christian faith when she
read his book, *Orthodoxy,* in her schooldays.

The club included a large representation of active crime

writers of the time, being made up of authors such as Agatha Christie, Ronald Knox, Freeman Wills Crofts, John Rhode, R. Austin Freeman, G.D.H. Cole, Margaret Cole, Helen Simpson, Eustace Robert Barton, E.C. Bentley, A.A. Milne, Baroness Orczy, Henry Wade, and H.C. Bailey. They were fellow mystery writers known to the innovative Anthony Berkeley Cox (initially writing as Anthony Berkeley[7]), who brightly suggested that they gather fairly regularly in London to eat and talk together, and to enjoy each other's company. The success of the gathering eventually was what soon led to the establishment of the Detection Club, which exists to this day. Berkeley might be said to have been the club's founder, which in fact Agatha Christie believed.[8] Also very active was the ever vivacious Sayers, who was to pour herself heavily into the group.

As the club solidified, it became apparent that it needed premises in which to meet, no doubt encouraged by Sayers' powerful enthusiasm and willingness to participate creatively in its workings, and also by the positivity of its members. Its home was to become 31, Gerrard Street, in London's commercial West End, replete with theatres, museums, art galleries, concert halls, university colleges and schools of art and of dance, churches, and much else.

Writing in *Strand Magazine* soon after the inauguration of the club, its first president, G.K. Chesterton, describes it as:

> ...in short, a small society of writers of detective stories; and its only object of amusing itself is best summed up in two statements: (1) That a detective story is a story, and subject to the same literary laws as a love story or a fairy story or any other form of literature; and (2) That the writer of a detective story is a writer; and is just as much bound in

> the sight of God and man to be a good writer,
> as if he were the writer of an epic or a tragedy.[9]

Of the group, Sayers was probably most informed about detective fiction, having been deeply interested in its nature and history while working at Ecole des Roches school in France with Eric Whelpton from 1919 to 1920 (see chapter 4). Toward the end of the 1920s her knowledge of the genre was formidable. When a newly established and greatly gifted publisher, Victor Gollancz, put it to her that she collect and edit an omnibus of short mystery stories, she took on the large project with relish.[10] Her long introduction to the collection turned out to be a groundbreaking overview of the history and character of tales of "detection, mystery, and horror". In particular, she was advanced in bringing together five, not just a usual three, stories of a pioneer of the genre, Edgar Allan Poe, which demonstrated, she pointed out, the connection between the three threads of detection, mystery, and horror. The five stories appeared between 1840 and 1845, and in her view the main ruling features of detective stories were set down. Since Poe, the three threads have abounded.[11]

The "general principles" Sayers referred to had been set out in 1928 in a way acceptable to many of the writers of mystery stories, popularly named as the "Decalogue" or "Ten Commandments of Detection", by a member of the Detection Club, Ronald Knox. Sayers at that time was rather seized by the strictures, like many in the club, before her detective stories broadened more into novels. She in fact became involved, probably with others, in composing initiation rules for new members of the club based on the "Decalogue". The script for the ceremony was entitled, "The Uncommon Order of Initiation of New Members of the Detection Club".

The ceremony became central to the club. It ordained

that with the assembling of the company, lights, presumably candle lights, would be extinguished, and the president of the club would proceed to the place of ceremony along with the presidential attendants and the candidates, following the designated order. Two torchbearers would lead, followed by an electronically illuminated human skull named Eric carried on a black cushion, and then next the secretary. The candidates would follow, with the sponsors holding torches, and then finally the president.

At the place of ceremony the president would cross-examine the candidates, beginning with the swearing of oaths, and election to the club – then the consequences of breaking the promises made would be read out.

At this time Sayers was to become a popular broadcaster on BBC Radio, as well as by then the well-known detective writer. The BBC introduced a radio play of hers, *The Footsteps that Ran*, with a typically brief paragraph in the *Radio Times*. The play was adapted by the BBC from one of her short stories featuring Lord Peter Wimsey. The BBC emphasized her seriousness over the accepted rules of such stories:

> As her many thousands of readers know,
> Dorothy L. Sayers is a detective-story writer who
> invariably plays fair. In *The Footsteps that Ran*,
> as in all her other ingenious stories, all clues to
> the identity of the murderer, the motive of the
> murderer, the weapon used, and the method of
> detection are suggested to the reader.[12]

Novelist P.D. James got more to the heart of the conventions used by writers of such stories in the Golden Age between the two world wars. She saw them as being marked "by a highly organised structure and recognised conventions" that separates the period from "mainstream fiction" and "the generality of crime stories". A main aim, she writes in her book *Talking About Detective Fiction*, is "the bringing of order out of disorder and the restoration of peace after the destructive eruption of murder". Its conservatism at least nominally confirms the belief "that we live in a rational, comprehensible and moral universe".[13]

The necessary funding for the club, the members decided, would come not from their financial contributions but from collaborations by them on serials for broadcast that could be collected into book-length publications. As chapters were written by members they were passed on to other members to continue the overall story in a kind of round robin. The instalments were first broadcast on BBC Radio, and then might appear in the weekly *Listener,* often with book publication after completion. Sayers was to contribute to a number of the series, with her enthusiasm and drive keeping other contributors to deadlines. The first of these ventures was titled *Behind the Screen,* and was broadcast in the early summer of 1930, with each author reading their episodes, which became the custom.

The Scoop followed, being broadcast during January to April 1931 by Sayers, Agatha Christie, E.C. Bentley, Anthony Berkeley, Freeman Wills Crofts, and Clemence Dane. After the airing of a full-length collaborative detective novel in 1931, *The Floating Admiral*,[14] a further series followed with *Ask a Policeman,* published as a book in 1933. In the latter, a powerful additional challenge was posed for the contributors: each had to take on one of the others' detectives. Anthony Berkeley, the original instigator of the club, for instance, energetically took on a daunting episode representing Sayers' Lord Peter Wimsey.

As president of the Detection Club, Chesterton was amused by the successful publication of *The Floating Admirable*:

Perhaps the most characteristic thing that
the Detection Club ever did was to publish
a detective story, which was quite a good
detective story, but the best things in which
could not possibly be understood by anybody
except the gang of criminals that had produced
it. It was called *The Floating Admiral*, and was
written somewhat uproariously in the manner
of one of those "paper games" in which each
writer in turn continues a story of which he
knows neither head nor tail. It turned out
remarkably readable, but the joke of it will
never be discovered by the ordinary reader;
for the truth is that almost every chapter thus
contributed by an amateur detective is a satire
on the personal peculiarities of the last amateur
detective. This, it will be sternly said, is not the
way to become a best-seller. It is a matter of
taste; but to my mind there is always a curious
tingle of obscure excitement in the works of
this kind which have remained here and there
in literary history; the sort of book that it is
even more enjoyable to write than to read.[15]

Not only was Sayers involved with fellow members of the
Detection Club in the round robin broadcasts of these crime
stories on BBC Radio, but through the 1930s was in a variety
of other broadcasts. She became something of a familiar voice
on the air.

At that time the *Radio Times* listed a popular radio
programme called *On the 9.20* in which the listener is introduced
to a handful of people in a train carriage, with sound effects
of train noises in the background. They discuss subjects that

are of topical or permanent interest, including war, the police, the younger generation, and the American point of view. The people in the carriage have included eminent people such as Sayers, E.M. Forster, Hilaire Belloc and Julian Huxley.

Another feature, listed toward the end of the 1930s, on a Christmas Day, was in a programme for women, entitled, *For you, madam*. The episode was entitled, "The Women at the Top", and the subject on that occasion was Dorothy L. Sayers.

Despite her professional success, Dorothy's private life was thwart with problems. At the centre of her difficulties was Mac's declining health, with its impact on his life and temperament. Sayers however empathized with the constant shadow of his wartime wounds. By 1928 Mac had lost full-time posts, such as being a correspondent for the *News of the World*, and was forced to freelance. This fitted well into their permanent move to Witham from London in 1929, which suited self-employment better. At that time he and Sayers took a holiday in Gatehouse of Fleet in Kirkcudbrightshire (now part of the region of Dumfries and Galloway, in the south-west of Scotland). This began a pattern of holidays based in the area, but with the couple staying at the fishing and artists' town of Kirkcudbright. The vacations undoubtedly had a positive effect on Mac's wellbeing. Sayers could see the artistic environment pleased Mac, with his growing absorption in painting and sketching. It also satisfied his love of fishing. Also, he clearly related to Scotland; his birth in Kirkwall, Orkney was felt as part of his identity.

An important result of those holidays was Sayers' 1931 novel *The Five Red Herrings,* a Lord Peter Wimsey mystery based on the area, even employing local railway timetables, and real places.[16] Her foreword to the book is a dedication to Joe Dignam, the landlord of the Anwoth Hotel, in which she points out to him that all the places in the novel are real ones. The original hardback even has a real map of the area "for use with

'The Five Red Herrings'". It indicates the place where the body of the murder victim, a local artist, was found. In the story, there were six suspects, fellow artists, who wished him dead.

Despite the interludes in Galloway, Sayers was beset with the difficulties of living with Mac in the golden years of her creation of detective stories. She still loved him, and tried to understand what he was going through. His unpredictable outbursts of temper and his lack of resistance to the appeal of the bottle was a Job-like challenge for Sayers. His memory losses added to the storms.[17] She confided to her cousin Ivy in February 1933 about how she wished his health was better. Mac was highly finnicky over what he ate, increasing his depression. Sayers saw that his being difficult overall was caused by the war. Sayers added that Mac's health was the main reason why the two of them were so often away in Galloway.

It was a great blessing for Sayers when the Witham household was visited by her Aunt Maud, mother of Margaret Leigh.[18] When Sayers' aged Aunt Mabel had been living in Sunnyside Cottage toward the end of her life, she had been a great peacemaker between the warring factions, Sayers and Mac, to the former's great relief. When Aunt Maud was staying some time later, she showed a similar ability to keep the peace. Maybe it was because both aunts were from, or married into, the Leigh side of Sayers' genealogy. Sayers' cousin Margaret at that time lived in the Scottish Highlands, writing and enjoying a rural existence, and had been joined there by her mother, with some persuasion. Aunt Maud took time away from Scotland to stay with her niece in Witham, in Christmas 1932 and then for six weeks early in 1934. Sayers enjoyed her company very much, which was probably mutual. Both were former students at Somerville College, which gave them much in common. Sayers wrote to Ivy Shrimpton about how she liked her Aunt Maud, a liking shared by Mac. Both Sayers and Mac appreciated her intelligence, her enjoyment of seeing people, and conversation. Sayers confided in Ivy that her animation must make it difficult for the aging woman to be forced to live so far away.

The darkest period for Sayers probably came when her doctor ordered her to rest. This was in late autumn 1933. She had to take three weeks off from all work, having a complete holiday. The previous April Sayers had recovered from an illness that had lasted about a year. The nature of the illness was not revealed. It was likely to have been connected with the difficulties of sharing her life with Mac, in his decline in health, and overwork. The illness was severe enough, at least at one point, for her to be unable to correct the proofs of her book, *Have His Carcase*.

The doctor's order came at a critical point in Sayer's life, where her relationship with Mac was at breaking point, and her health was in danger over stress and the place her work had taken in order for her to continue to function. It was necessary for her to consider whether or not to leave Mac, and the continuing implications of her son John Anthony in her life. Mac's previous wish to have him join their household had now gone rather dead, even though the child would soon bear his surname Fleming, after an informal adoption. Sayers was aware of how unworkable it would be to have John Anthony living with them, given Mac's unpredictability and stormy rages. She had to get away from Mac for a little while, at least, to think things through. She turned to one of her confidants, her reliable old friend, Muriel St Clare Byrne, from Somerville days, and now a distinguished historian and lecturer in drama. They decided on a brief driving holiday.

In one of her frequent letters to Ivy in November 1933, she apologized in a very brief and hurried one that all kinds of troubles had been filling her life, to do with finances, issues at home, and other things. She indicated to Ivy that she would be in the Oxford area near the end of November, and would call at The Sidelings cottage to see her over a matter she under-emphasizes as a "bit of business". She was going in fact to discuss the whole matter of John Anthony with her cousin, including the informal adoption of the child.

As they travelled around, Byrne had noticed that Sayers appeared to be very depressed. On Sunday, 26 November, they would have driven late in the afternoon through Woodstock to the north of Oxford, then turned off the Chipping Norton road into a labyrinth of country lanes to get to Westcott Barton, and Ivy's cottage. Muriel St Clare Byrne recalled them stopping at a small cottage in a village in the evening dark. Sayers briefly left Byrne in the car while she went into the cottage, then came out to invite her friend in. Bryne, who knew nothing of Sayers' child, met there a nine-year-old boy, soon to be ten, and with him an older child called Isobel. Byrne was not enlightened that John Anthony was Sayers' son, and in fact was not to discover this until a day after her friend's death. On that day, a man of thirty-three appeared and asked if she was Miss St Clare Byrne. After Byrne answered in the affirmative, the young man declared, "I am Dorothy Sayers' son. May I come in?"

In the cottage, Sayers was able to talk with her cousin Ivy about the "bit of business" presumably without it being within the hearing of Muriel St Clare Byrne. The subject was about a form of adoption which would give Sayers' son an official place in her life, and also allow him the surname "Fleming". A normal legal process was out of the question, as this would require a birth certificate revealing that Sayers was John Anthony's mother. The informal adoption was necessary for the requirements of the boy's entry into school, which was impending. Sayers had been planning that he would enter a reputable boarding school, after the many years he'd had being taught by Ivy Shrimpton, whose teaching of her charges in their early years was of high quality. Ivy agreed to signing the necessary papers that would soon be sent to her. When the adoption took place, along with being given his new surname, John Anthony would be instructed to call Sayers "mummy" or "mother" and refer to Mac hence forward as his father.[19] He soon decided that he would be called "Anthony Fleming" rather than "John Anthony Fleming". This led to some calling him "Tony". The boy was nearly ready for school life, in his mother's view, who also had now made a resolution with herself during the brief motoring holiday that she would remain with Mac until parted by death. She was thankful when Mac agreed to the quasi-adoption of her son.

As the car drove off into the night from Ivy's cottage, its headlights constantly seeking in the dark the winding road ahead, Muriel St Clare Byrne noticed and would ever remember the tears on her friend's face.

8

FROM PAGE TO STAGE: TELLING THE GREATEST STORY (1936–51)

Dorothy Sayers, alas, has wearied of the
detective story and has turned her attention
elsewhere.

Agatha Christie[1]

Early in 1935 Sayers was making very real progress with an
untypical crime story which lacked a corpse, but which
contained sinister goings-on threatening an Oxford women's
college. It would be published by November that year. What
became *Gaudy Night* was, unusually for the author, declaring
a moral message relating to the matter of her intellectual
integrity[2], the sacrament (as she saw it) of work, and passionate
scholarship. As was her habit, through the writing of *Gaudy
Night* Sayers would be working on several books at once, not
always being fiction, as changes in her publications later in the
decade show.

In her biographical book, *The Women at Oxford,* Vera Brittain
points to changes ahead for Sayers:

For the writing of *Gaudy Night* – a thriller
based on a women's college and published in

> 1935 – she spent long periods at Somerville
> [College]. But two years later she gave up
> detective fiction altogether and returned, as
> she could now afford, to her real love – the
> study of theology as manifested in the precise
> dogmas of Anglo-Catholicism.[3]

Central to Sayers' beliefs was that theology, as she saw it, was
not humourless. It was while thoroughly into writing *Gaudy
Night* that her deeply embedded sense of humour and fun lit up
her gift of seeing beyond gloom and the weary difficulties of life.
She would turn to writing another story involving Harriet Vane,
a venture into drama, while still working on *Gaudy Night*. A
sweep had been called to clean the chimneys at her Essex home,
Sunnyside Cottage. As he worked away on the winter's day
Sayers became more and more interested in how he undertook
the job. He had come to Sayers' Witham house wearing several
layers of pullovers. To her fascination, as he warmed up during
his labours he would remove one of the pullovers, then after
a while another, then another, gradually going through all the
layers. Adding to the spectacle was the colourful patterns of the
pullovers as they were revealed. The image of the sweep at work
remained in her mind's vision, and would make her smile or
laugh as she remembered or spoke of the experience. Perhaps
she recalled the way Sir Hugh Allen, when conducting the Bach
Choir, had the habit of discarding some of his clothes in the
heat of action.[4]

Soon after the sweeping of the chimneys Sayers visited
her close friends Muriel St Clare Byrne, and her companion,
Marjorie Barber, in their shared house in the St John's Wood
area of London, a place she had often visited. Like Byrne,
Marjorie Barber, known as "Bar", was a friend going back to
the jubilant university days of the Mutual Admiration Society.

Unable to restrain her laughter, Sayers told them of the recent visitation of the many-pullovered sweep. Aware of Byrne's deep knowledge of the stage, an interest shared by Bar and herself, she added that the sweep would make a dazzling character and she would like to place him in a play. The way the sweep spoke was also as captivating to her as his apparent strip-teasing. Byrne responded by asking Sayers, "Why don't *you* do it, then?" From this seed was to grow a whole new development in the creativity of one who was known worldwide as a leading voice of the Golden Age of crime fiction.

Sayers had not been able to ignore this suggestion early in 1935 from her friend. Byrne, who was not only deeply knowledgeable of the theatre, but also its history. Like Sayers, Byrne worked in many areas. She took seriously her own work as Elizabethan scholar, dramatist specializing in Elizabethan theatre, and a literary critic. Just one of the aspects of her life was to take on the gargantuan task of editing for publication the *Lisle Letters*, which ran into a correspondence by Arthur Plantagenet, 1st Viscount Lisle, of around 3,000 letters (a formidable number similar to the quantity of letters Sayers was to write that were eventually published). They were published in six volumes in 1981, two years before her death.

Some days following the meeting when Sayers had been challenged by Byrne, she wrote rather light-headedly to her friend, from her London apartment, describing a striking coincidence that she felt Byrne ought to know about. Sayers recounted seeing not one, but two, portents that really struck her. That morning when she had ventured out on some business she encountered a chimney sweep. It seemed to her a good omen. Later, when she returned to Great James Street, she noticed through her window a man passing by bearing a clean set of the usual chimney sweep tools. She had never before seen such a vision, it being so rare, she considered.

Dropping the humorous tone, Sayers continued in the letter, with her characteristic and perhaps deliberately exaggerated detail, to describe the murder-machine she had researched to be part of the stage set in the drama they were now writing together.[5]

In the story, the comic side of the murder mystery really starts to unfold as the honeymooners, Lord Peter and Harriet Vane, encounter a succession of unexpected mishaps when they arrive at their new home, "Tallboys", in Fen country. Everything seems to go wrong and, even worse, a corpse is eventually discovered in the cellar. Not surprisingly, to her friends involved in creating the play, Sayers nicknamed the new home, "Calamity Cottage".

The play and subsequent novel were to provide an effective denouement for the drawn-out saga of Lord Peter's quest for the hand in marriage of Harriet, the detective story writer; a solution to the resolving of the romance which Sayers had sought for a long time. She complained to Byrne that the pair were decidedly ungainly lovers, over-sensitive and averse to commitments unless conveyed indirectly. In a pattern within Sayers' rich torrent of murder mysteries, which began with *Whose Body?* in 1923, are a number of books over seven years featuring Harriet Vane along with Lord Peter, perhaps echoing the biblical Jacob's long quest for his love Rachel (though with no equivalent of Leah).

Many readers, including Sayers' friend Agatha Christie (and even J.R.R. Tolkien, whose work she admired), were not amused by her development of the crime story into novel, and her going to even greater depth in her stories with a complex love interest.[6] Agatha Christie commented:

> Dorothy Sayers, alas, has wearied of the
> detective story and has turned her attention

elsewhere. We all regret it for she was such an exceptionally good detective story writer and a delightfully witty one. Her earlier books *Whose Body?*, *Unnatural Death* and *The Unpleasantness at the Bellona Club* are decidedly her best, having greater simplicity and more "punch" to them. Also her detective "Lord Peter Wimsey", whose face was originally piquantly described as "emerging from his top hat like a maggot emerging from a gorgonzola cheese", became through the course of years merely a "handsome hero", and admirers of his early prowess can hardly forgive his attachment to, and lengthy courtship of, a tiresome young woman called Harriet. One had hoped that, once married to her, he would resume his old form, but Lord Peter remains an example of a good man spoilt.[7]

There was certainly some controversy over Sayers' change of approach in her detective stories which Agatha Christie had highlighted. Tolkien in his turn made decidedly negative comments about Sayers' later crime novels in a private letter:

I could not stand *Gaudy Night*. I followed P[eter Wimsey] from his attractive beginnings so far, by which time I conceived a loathing for him (and his creatrix) not surpassed by any other character in literature known to me, unless by his Harriet [Vane]. The honeymoon one (*Busman's H.*?) was worse. I was sick....[8]

Clearly, Tolkien had enjoyed Sayers' earlier stories featuring Lord Peter Wimsey, but not the later stories which had a love interest with a writer of crime stories, Harriet Vane. These belonged to a period when Sayers was impressively developing her detective stories into literary novels. *Gaudy Night* (1935) in fact is often now considered one of her great novels.

In contrast to Christie and Tolkien, eminent theologian Ann Loades CBE points to Sayers' novel's quality and topicality:

> [*Gaudy Night*] is both a detective story and
> an unabashed defence of academic and
> intellectual work as undertaken by women,
> for whom she was a provocative advocate
> throughout her life. In her detective fiction
> she explored the emotional cost to Wimsey
> and others of establishing the truth about the
> circumstances of the various deaths of her
> fictional characters, and she also explored the
> mediation of impartial divine justice through
> the relatively imperfect procedures of the rule
> of law in the society of her day.[9]

Another Wimsey story that is considered great is her *The Nine Tailors* (1934), in which Harriet Vane does not in fact appear but a deep love of accomplished church bell-ringing certainly does. In its greatness it is far from Agatha Christie's "simplicity" but, for many readers, succeeds in having "punch".

The popular theatre production of *Busman's Honeymoon* was to provide a dramatic conclusion to the romance between Lord Peter and Harriet, with the couple's marriage and eventful honeymoon. Perhaps Sayers began to see more clearly that theatre could provide a declaration of fulfilment in the case of the lovers more powerfully than could a novel.[10]

Sayers and Muriel St Clare Byrne worked together until Easter to complete the three-act play, which would appear on the London stage on 16 December 1936. It then ran for nine months, turning out to be an enormous success with a large number of performances.

Sayers' son Anthony, nearly thirteen, had started boarding in autumn 1936 at a preparatory school in Broadstairs, Kent, and he and his mother were writing to each other more frequently. Near the end of October, she wrote an exuberant letter to him about frantic preparations for putting on *Busman's Honeymoon* in Birmingham early in November. Sayers had arranged for Anthony to attend a performance.

The hurly burly of theatre, with writing plays and being thoroughly involved in the production, stimulated Sayers enormously, after the long hours of writing her detective stories, often penned in a stressful home life, as Mac's infirmities continued to develop. As long as two years before, Sayers had included a heavily disturbing event in one of her frequent letters to Ivy. She told her cousin that a most odd and upsetting event had happened at home, relating to Mac. Sayers had got back after being in London for a while and discovered an important letter from Ivy among other letters that Mac had totally forgotten to send on to her, or even to mention them to her. This example of Mac's oddness and lack of reliability illustrated more and more frequent unusual behaviour on his part, so much so that it was unsafe to trust him with anything. Sayers added to Ivy in her letter that whenever she informed him he had forgotten anything he would explode in an alarming rage. Doctors had agreed that he was getting increasingly odd, leading Sayers to consider that there was little that could be done about it.[11]

Following the initial Birmingham productions of the *Busman's Honeymoon* play and its opening in London at the Comedy Theatre in December, by the next June her novel, based closely on the play, and having the same name, was published. (Its first edition, published in New York, came out in

February 1937.) Apart from some short stories, Sayers stopped writing detection mysteries with *Busman's Honeymoon*, though she did leave an unfinished and abandoned crime novel called *Thrones, Dominations*, which was completed after her death, at the request of Sayer's estate, by the novelist Jill Paton Walsh.

However, Sayers did create a brief series of wartime pieces, reflecting her interests and concerns and showing some continuity between the old and new: these were published in *The Spectator* from November 1939 to January 1940 and titled "The Wimsey Papers". They took the form of correspondence between Wimsey family members and other characters known to avid readers of the Lord Peter Wimsey novels. Sayers' idea behind the letters was to air her opinions and observations on public life in the opening months of the Second World War. The issues incorporated blackouts, evacuation, the imposition of rationing, and the obligation of the public to take personal responsibility instead of waiting around for guidance from the government. The letter-writers' opinions ranged from down-to- earth and specific advice on such issues as how pedestrians can avoid being struck by vehicles in the blackout to far-seeing ideas for a post-war reconstruction of Britain. Sayers had long been wrestling with the issues of rebuilding British society after a world war before the Second World War even started, rather as her acquaintance[12] T.S. Eliot had endeavoured, in 1939, to pose the idea of a Christian society and culture in his *The Idea of a Christian Society and Other Writings*.[13] It was all part of Sayers feeling her way after leaving behind her crown as eminent writer of detection and mystery novels. As with others, T.S. Eliot would be drawn to Sayers' creativity. Theologian Ann Loades points out: "Her work was of considerable interest to authors as different as T.S. Eliot..., C.S. Lewis..., and Charles Williams...."[14]

C.S. Lewis, as a friend, prepared a panegyric for Sayers which was read at her memorial service in 1957, and which throws some light on why she turned from writing detective fiction. He wrote:

> Prigs have put it about that Dorothy in later
> life was ashamed of her "tekkies" and hated
> to hear them mentioned. A couple of years
> ago my wife [Joy Davidman Lewis] asked her
> if this was true and was relieved to hear her
> deny it. She had stopped working in that genre
> because she felt she had done all she could
> with it. And indeed, I gather, a full process of
> development had taken place.[15]

It had been somewhere roughly between 1936 and 1938 that Sayers took the visibly different route as an author. Her turn from writing detective fiction in favour of a variety of lay theology, included ways of defending or re-establishing Christian belief, often in her essays or in a groundbreaking book like *The Mind of the Maker* (1941), and in writing plays usually with a religious element. There could be several reasons for this, such as that she may have realized that the ethos underpinning detective fiction of the Golden Age was losing its claims over readers. Christian belief, and the creeds which had given moral and intellectual stability, she discovered, needed defending and celebrating.

Writing and then helping to produce *Busman's Honeymoon* had undoubtedly awakened something in Sayers. The world of theatre was in fact pointing her to a cultural shift which, though perhaps minor, had a welcome place for her and her creativity, even given her already enormous international status in the world of detection fiction. She was then drawn in by an invitation, just as the challenge of Muriel St Clare Byrne earlier had compelled her into new territory.

There was a thread behind the invitation, which was formed by some of those who had become aware of how gifted and innovative Sayers was. The thread went back a long way. If opposition to her poetry in *Catholic Tales and Christian Songs*, published just before the armistice in 1918, had been mentioned to her, she would no doubt have recalled how an unusual writer and poet had come to her defence over her writing.[16] This remarkable person was Charles Williams, who in particular had liked a poetic drama of hers which was rather in the manner of a mystery play, "The Mocking of Christ: A Mystery", when it had appeared in *Catholic Tales* around twenty years before. Williams would one day in the distant future be remembered by close friends as a "poet, novelist, critic, and incomparable talker" with a "darting, fantastic, and challenging intellect".[17] In *The Times'* obituary just days after Williams' death in 1945, T.S. Eliot would write warmly of him. When Williams had for a period conducted evening tutorial classes, Eliot observed that the lively lecturer enraptured his audiences with his enthusiastic outpouring, which excelled itself in extensive quotation from literature that he loved. His powerful yet humble personality was fervent with goodness itself, winning the hearts of his students, inspiring a love for the literature he taught.[18] Charles Williams was much more than a talkative, highly intelligent writer, as Sayers was to find when she got to know him in person as a friend, and much later wrote voluminous letters to him regarding their deep, shared interests.

Charles Williams was to return again to Sayers' perception via her publisher and friend Victor Gollancz around fifteen years later in 1933. Over the years that followed she would meet up informally on a number of occasions with the charismatic Williams. Gollancz had sent Williams, who frequently reviewed crime stories, a copy of Sayers' latest Wimsey story, *The Nine*

Tailors, before publication.[19] Gollancz immediately quoted Williams' glorious response to the novel in a letter to the author. In it, Williams complimented its imagination, particularly praising the preludes, and ended by saying that he didn't think Sayers would be able to top it.

After these encouraging comments to her publisher, the thread continued dramatically for Sayers. Williams had developed a strong contact with the Canterbury Festival. This drama festival was an important part in what was gradually taking place widely as a minor renewal of a Christian presence in British contemporary culture. Though no one knows exactly why Sayers stopped writing mystery fiction in the mid-1930s, certainly her promising Wimsey play, *Busman's Honeymoon*, would kindle an interest in her work for the Canterbury Festival, which would lead to her writing her impressive drama, *The Zeal of Thy House* (1937) for it. Here Charles Williams' influence had come in once more. His long-standing appreciation of her mystery poem, "The Mocking of Christ", in the style of a medieval mystery play, and her novel, *The Nine Tailors,* led him to approach the Canterbury Festival. He had been commissioned by the festival to write *Thomas Cranmer of Canterbury* (1936) to follow T.S. Eliot's *Murder in the Cathedral* (1935). Williams suggested to Canterbury that they approach Sayers for a festival play, which they did. Her success with *Busman's Honeymoon* in a London West End theatre, from its very opening, would have been an encouraging factor, not only for reinforcing the festival's choice of Sayers, but also for her necessary confidence needed for creating a play timed for 1937! By February the prolific writer had made good progress.

The very existence of the Canterbury Festival was an important marker of change in the air. George Bell, then Dean of Canterbury Cathedral, decided to help to bring theatre back into the church, picking up a great tradition that had been forced into neglect. He instituted the Canterbury Festival, which soon attracted a following. In the English church, the prohibitions against acting in churches, which had survived from the time of Oliver Cromwell, were lifted with Bell's launch of the festival. From Easter 1918, however, the very first English church from the time of the Reformation to give a home to religious plays, and a welcoming one at that, was St Silas the Martyr in Kentish Town, London, attended by Charles Williams and family.[20] The Canterbury Festival's own productions were to become many and varied, including plays by John Masefield, as well as T.S. Eliot, Charles Williams, and, by 1937, the play in preparation by Sayers. Williams himself had come to Bishop Bell's attention when he was editing at Oxford University Press the bishop's two-volume biography of Randall Davidson, Archbishop of Canterbury.

T.S. Eliot, Charles Williams, Graham Greene, and others, along with Sayers, would have a cultural impact during the 1930s and 1940s. Charles Williams was bringing out literary criticism and supernatural thrillers such as *The Place of the Lion,* which Lewis, Tolkien, and others of their friends read and discussed around 1936, boosting their own fiction. In 1940 W.H. Auden began composing his poem "New Year Letter" under the influence of Williams' highly unusual history of the church, *The Descent of the Dove,* which had been published the year before.

In an article about C.S. Lewis, literary historian and critic, Harry Blamires expanded on some more of the authors who were part of what he had called a minor literary renaissance, clearly indicating its importance, nevertheless. He concluded:

> So when the literary historian looks back at the
> English literary scene in the 1930s and 1940s he
> is going to see C.S. Lewis and Charles Williams,

not as freakish throwbacks, but as initial
contributors to what I have called a Christian
literary renaissance, and a minor one.[21]

Sayers in that period was to become friends with both Lewis
and Williams, whom Blamires called "initial contributors" to
the modest movement, becoming an important contributor
herself.

The part played, often indirectly, by Williams over many
years in Sayers' eventual writing of the play *The Zeal of Thy
House* for the Canterbury Festival, led her to make contact with
Lewis, at first by letter. Since 1936 Williams had begun to have
a very important impact on Lewis, before he also came to have
a huge impact upon Sayers' thought and writing.

Meanwhile, John Anthony Fleming, who preferred to be
known as "Anthony Fleming", was doing very well at school,
and would eventually achieve a place at Balliol College at
Oxford in 1941, though war service with the Technical Branch
of the Royal Air Force would delay his studies for several years.
Sayers' humour would have been tickled as Balliol was the
place at which her creation, Lord Peter Wimsey, had studied
while recovering from the psychological scars of war. Also,
the chaplain there was none other than Maurice Roy Ridley,
who had long before, as a wartime Oxford student, been an
inspiration in her creation of Wimsey, in appearance at least.
While working on the script of *Busman's Honeymoon* with Muriel
St Clare Byrne and Marjorie Barber, Sayers had been stunned
in early March 1935 by meeting the physical "Wimsey" while
coming across again Ridley in Oxford, not remembering him as
the student long ago who had entranced her. In a letter straight
after the shock, composed in the Bodleian Library, Sayers wrote
dramatically to Byrne in that silent place about her broken heart
as a result of seeing in many respects a real life Lord Peter, then

learning the bruising fact that Ridley was very different in being Balliol College's chaplain! The humour was there again when Ridley was set to become Anthony's tutor at the time her son was accepted to study at the college.

* * * * *

When Sayers was commissioned to write a play for the Canterbury Festival, due for 1937, she clearly realized that time for creating it was limited, based on her experience of writing *Busman's Honeymoon* that time with the help of Byrne and Barber.

With Canterbury itself in mind, Margaret Babington of the Friends of Canterbury Cathedral had asked her to base the drama on a French architect who had been chosen to rebuild part of the cathedral that had been badly damaged in a great fire in 1174, following the murder of Thomas à Becket (the subject of T.S. Eliot's *Murder in the Cathedral*).

William of Sens is a gifted architect of wide experience who becomes crippled by pride over his achievements, to the extent of being blind, as a maker, to how much he is helped in his work – and indeed has to be helped – by the Divine Maker. He attributes all his successes to himself, not to what he has been given. Literally, his pride comes before a fall, when a frayed rope, to which he is attached while working high up, gives way. Consequently, he is permanently crippled. Describing the disaster, a monk named Gervase, who carefully recorded in Latin the years of rebuilding and William's fall, links it with "either the vengeance of God or the envy of the Devil, wreaked itself on him alone".[22] There is an element of Faustus, of rendering one's self to the devil, to Sayer's telling of the events in the light of Gervase's Latin historical record. Her next drama for the festival, in 1939 would be, *The Devil to Pay*, in which the supernatural element of the famous Dr Faustus legend becomes the story, relevant, she felt, to the pre-war climate of the late 1930s.

Around the time Sayers was finishing her draft of *The Zeal of Thy House* in February 1937, she describes in a letter an unembarrassed Charles Williams, in great excitement, reading a passage from the play loudly, continually bouncing up and down on his seat, in Simpson's, a rather exclusive London restaurant.[23] The passage she refers to Charles Williams reading is William of Sens' blasphemous speech of what she sees as concluding with a blast of pride of the worst kind, that is, from a proud spirit. The passage begins with William asserting that both God and himself were equally master-craftsmen, who understood each other. It was only he who could sense God's heartbeat during the ancient days of the beginning of creation. William goes on to declare that in creating humankind God went too far, and parted with his very divinity: he became dependent on man.

In contrast is the positive ending of *The Zeal of Thy House*, where the archangel Michael (traditionally, the adversary of Lucifer), addresses the congregation in the cathedral's Chapter House, with other angels standing above him. Michael's powerful address also leads on to another of Sayers' works – a book, not a play. *The Mind of the Maker*, published 1941, is one of the greatest of this rich period, for Sayers, of exploring Christian teaching as relevant to contemporary life. Michael, presenting the opposite to William of Sens, magnificently celebrates human beings as bearing the image of God the creator, rather than being God's equal. He renders human beings as makers and craftsman, as the creator is, but only as little but magnificent reflections of his triune majesty, the majesty of his Trinity.

Michael, the archangel, continues his speech with the message that every act of human creation is in three – to reflect on earth the heavenly Trinity. He declares that the creative idea is first, viewing the complete work at once, the end in the beginning (the image of the Father); next is the creative energy, expressed from that idea, working out throughout time from beginning to end, embodying the real (the image of the Word); finally, there is the creative power, the work's meaning and its response in the living soul (the image of the Spirit that indwells). The three are equally one, equally the complete work, equally existing with the others (the image of the Trinity). Thus Michael beautifully expresses the earthly trinity in the play's finale. In her later *The Mind of the Maker*, Sayers extensively explores the rich analogy between God and the human in our creative work, which has inspired many readers to this day.

Contemporary theologian, John Thurmer, who has written knowledgably on Sayers' thinking about the Trinity, has also drawn his readers' attention to R.C. Moberly, who wrote while Sayers was a young girl, seeking, like she later would, ideas of the earthly trinity in the image of God, in a concrete way:

> First, then, there is the man as he really is in himself, invisible, indeed, and inaccessible – and yet, directly, the fountain, origin, and cause of everything that can be called in any sense himself. Secondly, there is himself as projected into conditions of visibleness – the overt expression or utterance of himself. This, under the conditions of our actual experience, will mean for the most part his expression or image as body – the touch of his hand, the tone of his voice, the shining of his eye, the utterance of his words: all, in a word, that makes up, to us, that outward expression of himself, which we call himself, and which he

> himself ordinarily recognizes as the very mirror
> and image and reality of himself. And thirdly,
> there is the reply of what we call external
> nature to him – his operation or effect.[24]

While Moberly wrote of the heavenly Trinity being embedded in the human person, Sayers' much later emphasis was on human work, revealing the Trinity in the creative divine image in humans. John Thurmer points out that Moberley was "looking for analogies of the Spirit, and omits to say that the inner self and the revealed self are analogies of the Father and the Son, though it cannot be doubted that such was his intention".[25] Sadly, Moberly never expanded his brief, brilliant insight. There is no evidence that Sayers knew of his writings. We can only imagine how it might have increased her groundbreaking thinking on the Trinity and its image in creative work.

Before the writing of the prose treatise, *The Mind of the Maker*, the core of which is briefly captured in the archangel Michael's powerful address to the congregation, Sayers wrote her follow-on play, *The Devil to Pay,* for the 1939 Canterbury Festival. In the meantime, she managed a tour of *The Zeal of Thy House,* enjoying theatre production as much as the writing of drama. When the play first appeared at the Canterbury Festival, Sayers had enthusiastically arranged a trip to the production and reception for a private party of acquaintances and her friends, including Helen Simpson and her distinguished surgeon husband, the inseparable Muriel St Clare Byrne and Marjorie Barber, Mr and Mrs Scott-Giles (who helped to develop a detailed history of Lord Peter's ancestry), and her favourite Aunt Maud (her late mother's sister). She herself had to be in Canterbury for the dress rehearsal, so arranged for her secretary, a Miss Lake, to meet "the pilgrims" at lunchtime at Victoria Station to guide them to her especially booked Canterbury train, on the day of the opening performance. To help the travellers to find her secretary, Sayers arranged for her to conspicuously carry a copy of *Busman's Honeymoon* with the distinct bright yellow jacket of the Gollancz edition. On the train, a meal was provided. After the performance there was a "Service of Arts and Crafts" in the cathedral, celebrating the religious nature of an artist's work. The entrance of local mayors from the region was followed by a procession made up of architects, writers, painters, sculptors, and musicians, with Sayers among them.

Mac Fleming was notably absent from the performance and events. There were others Sayers desired to be present, such as further members of the Mutual Admiration Society like Dorothy Rowe of Bournemouth, an avid lover of theatre, who could not be there.

* * * * *

There is much to be said of this important period of Sayers' life, including mainly religious drama, but also, just as fittingly, a light-hearted play, *Love All* (1940), and, with her BBC experience, her invitation more fully into mainstream BBC Radio theatre. Consonant with drama were her lay writings which celebrated the deeper drama of the creeds and teaching of Christianity, underpinned by historical narrative, telling the greatest story of all. This was a story of catastrophe, followed by the happiest ending of all endings.

As well as retelling historical stories, she also translated imagined stories from long ago from some of the greatest poets. Sayers also captured important changes of her times, such as the slowly achieved emancipation of women, which was creating a foundation of hope. This hope was for so many who were held back by the ideas of others, ideas that were unfit to stand up to the scrutiny of accurate and properly thought-out theology. For

Sayers such theology was the central reality of both men and women being made in the image of God – as is every person irrespective of colour and wealth, status and health. Some of her lively essays became famous as ahead of her time, like "Are Women Human?"

She also boldly explained in an article in a book intended for senior school children how there is a definite evil power in the world. The article was entitled, "Is there a definite evil power that attacks people in the same way as there is a good power that influences people?" One of the themes in her response to the question was that the evil power thrived on division and destruction. Another was that the evil spirit, unable to create anything, could only turn to use its will to seize something that was good, and twist and bend it into ugliness. Rather than difference being a good thing – as the skin colour of people or the differences between man and woman – the evil power could distort such differences into division and hatred. Even the differences between humankind and the earth could be turned into destruction and unrestrained exploitation. Her article prepared her way for concluding that wherever there is degradation of humans and animal species, and tearing to pieces of natural ecologies, there you find Satan. The evil spirit who could create nothing has destruction as its signature.

The article is an example of her ability to communicate effectively, and to be ahead of her time in her understanding of pressing issues such as misuse of the environment, and other less discussed evils.[26] Like C.S. Lewis in his wartime BBC Radio broadcasts, Sayers, a popular broadcaster herself, is difficult to match in lucidity, and in using vivid images and metaphors to prevent communication being too abstract. Writing for the school children was a challenge she took on with apparent ease. She wrestled the issue of sin and of evil, which has been discussed for thousands of years, in a remarkably fresh way.

9

A NEW LOVE: REBOOTING DANTE AND THE DIVINE COMEDY (1944–57)

> After the start of the Second World War,
> however, she turned her attention away from
> crime writing. Focusing on the translation of
> Dante, and writing about religious subjects....
> But [she] remained associated with the
> Detection Club... holding the office of
> President from 1948 until her death.
>
> **Martin Edwards' foreword to *Ask a Policeman*[1]**

As Sayers saw an impending world war toward the end of the 1930s, and the pressing need to work out how to rebuild society when war was over, she continued a theme of her Canterbury play, *The Zeal of Thy House* – the birth and development of evil, which was so evident in contemporary fascism and popularism. She decided that her next play for the Canterbury Festival would be around the famous legend of Dr Faustus, told on the Elizabethan stage by Christopher Marlowe, by Goethe in his play, and in other ways, such as in its influence upon Mikhail Bulgakov's classic Russian novel, *The Master and Margarita* (published in 1966, and much translated). She was not alone in what she saw.

C.S. Lewis had pictured the attacks of hell on the human soul in a brilliant map of the world of thought in the 1920s and early 1930s in his story *The Pilgrim's Regress* (1933), and then more accessibly in his very successful, *The Screwtape Letters* (1942), which Sayers admired. His concern over devilry and the spiritual battles that face everyone were shared by other writers he knew of his time, and there were more stories he wrote exposing the dark side. His friend Tolkien had had the Dark Lord lurking in the gloomy haunts of Mirkwood in his *The Hobbit*, published in 1937, who would become better known as Sauron in the later *The Lord of the Rings*. Charles Williams, befriended by Lewis in 1936, had been writing stories of devilry for years. This is why Sayers, with her similar concerns, turned her attention to one of the definitive stories of selling one's soul to the devil, which was the pact that Dr Faustus had made with Satan. That was in her 1939 play for the Canterbury Festival, *The Devil to Pay*. Her play enriched the wide exploration of modern and ancient devilry in the writings of Lewis and his friends, as well as others.[2] She would later turn to writing a new translation of Dante's three volumes of *The Divine Comedy*, complete with extensive introductions, commentaries, brief summaries of each canto, and diagrams of the imagined worlds of hell, purgatory, and paradise.

Sayers turned the Faustus story into her own play, performed shortly before the Second World War, because of its relevance, she felt, to the powers and forces leading the world toward destruction. As a leading author in the Golden Age of murder mysteries – the interwar period – her characters Lord Peter Wimsey and Harriet Vane of course were widely known. These detective stories implied a general acceptance of Jewish-Christian values. Writing the Faustus play continued her decision in effect to abandon her successful detective writing, in exchange for drama and lay theology – theology written for a general readership. She wished to tackle the growing ignorance of what Lewis was later to call "Old Western" values in contemporary society. At that later time, she would identify with Lewis as a "fellow dinosaur". Lewis was not alone, therefore, in his increasing preoccupation with devilry and the dangers we face in trying to live a life marked by goodness rather than badness. Both he and Sayers, it seems, saw their time as facing powers that seemed bent on destroying our very humanity, and before which we can feel helpless. Of Sayers' writings on Christian belief for her cultural and social context, theologian Professor Ann Loades concludes: "Eurocentric, western, and written out of and in response to major social and political crises – Dorothy L. Sayers nevertheless makes it possible for us to recognize the importance of Christian dogma, how we receive it, and how we transmit it."[3]

Sayers creatively reworked the legend of Faustus, and included the standard characters such as Wagner, the demon Mephistopheles, and Helen of Troy. Her challenge was to bring in a natural human version of a more than human legend.[4] In her preface she points out that the great Faustus legend embodies the ultimate dilemma: the character of evil, and where it fits into the universe. If evil is symbolized in the devil, how did the devil come to be? In its opposition to God, is it equal to God (the ancient Manichean view)? What does it mean for a person to sell their soul to the devil? What kind of person would do so? What would induce them to do it? How does the devil relate to ideas of hell and damnation? Every new generation, she decided, has to answer such questions according to its experience of evil, and the spiritual needs that are part of that generation.

Sayers own take on the story is to depart from Goethe's warning against the fervent pursuit of knowledge for its own sake, which she concluded was not our big problem. Rather, she took up what she saw as the modern phenomenon of the reformer led by impulse, disliking the impediment of facts, and possessed by the need to instantly sort out the world by quick domination. A reformer, she felt, eventually falls into defeatism and escapes from reality. It is intriguing that such a reformer is to be found in her friend C.S. Lewis' early narrative poem, *Dymer* (1926), with Dymer's ideas kindling bloody revolution. (Lewis was very aware of the intellectual cross-currents of the period between the two world wars.) The form the modern reformer's escape takes, believed Sayers, was frequent in her time (she writes in the late 1930s, of course, with tyrants at loose in Germany, Italy, Spain, and Russia, and with catastrophic war impending). Evil could not be undone, she believed, as if periods of time could be reversed, but only purged, and redeemed by Christ in history. This, as it were, could be the only happy ending for human history.

* * * * *

Just before the Second World War, as the world faced catastrophe, J.R.R. Tolkien had given a historic lecture on the fairy tale at St Andrew's University in Scotland. At its core he introduced a new word which he saw as at the heart of great story. The word is "eucatastrophe" – the *good* catastrophe. Then unknown to Tolkien, the word fittingly expressed a pattern that lay behind the two creations that were particularly important in the later years of Sayers' life from wartime until her untimely death in 1957: one was her wartime BBC Radio drama series, *The Man Born to Be King,* and the other her translation from old Italian of Dante's masterpiece, *The Divine Comedy*, for a newly created imprint of Penguin paperback books – *Penguin Classics*. The pattern of both was the eucatastrophe. In *The Man Born to Be King* there was the truly happy ending of the resurrection of Christ, and in *The Divine Comedy* there was the final vision of Paradise and of the figure of Beatrice after her lover Dante's successful guided journey through hell and purgatory.

It is unlikely that Sayers came across the word "eucatastrophe" before 1947, when Tolkien's lecture appeared in print, and filled out, in the chapter "On Fairy-Stories" in *Essays Presented to Charles Williams*. The book was created as a memorial from friends of Charles Williams, such as Sayers. Williams died shortly after V.E. Day in 1945, and the editor of the memorial, C.S. Lewis, had soon asked Sayers to contribute. Her essay appears first in the book and is entitled "…And Telling you a Story, a Note on *The Divine Comedy*". C.S. Lewis' essay-contribution to the book was also on stories, with his preface to the book introducing Charles Williams, joining the efforts of others elsewhere, who knew Williams, such as T.S. Eliot, W.H. Auden, John Heath Stubbs, Anne Ridler, Alice Mary Hadfield, and Dorothy Sayers, to explain the remarkable man who had touched their lives.

Though Sayers would not have come across Tolkien's essay until after the memorial was published in 1947, before then much of Sayers' creativity was taken up with plays, essays, and books that communicated Christian faith in a contemporary setting. This however did mean her seeing the creation of the universe as good, with what has gone wrong with the world being the result of what has gone wrong with human beings. The state of the world and the misuse of what is good is a tragedy, but its story of redemption is the reversal and hallowing of catastrophe into good catastrophe – eucatastrophe. Here good has come out of what declares itself a catastrophe and a tragedy. Her writings do pick up the happy ending, while realistically portraying the state of the world. Her dramas at this time do so, but also her essays, and her seminal book on the divine pattern behind human creativity, *The Mind of the Maker*: seeing the human as being in God's image, which importantly includes creating as an image bearer of God, even though flawed in bearing the image. She describes her book as really having to do with representing Christian dogma about God, by drawing an analogy with the essential character of the creative mind of the artist. What Sayers takes from the drama and excitement of Christian "dogma", that is, "teaching", fundamentally has the same pattern as Tolkien's in exploring the making of great stories. It is significant that Sayers could thoroughly enjoy reading Tolkien's *The Lord of the Rings,* when it came out in the 1950s, and presumably his medieval scholarship, and it is likely she would have relished his then unknown translations of medieval writings, as a fervent translator herself.

In his 1947 version of his essay on fairy stories, Tolkien was essentially asking whether, in the telling of stories, can a catastrophe be good, if the stories follow the pattern of reality itself? As his friend C.S. Lewis asked himself, can myth become fact, or can fact be portrayed effectively in myth?

Tolkien's Christian faith lies behind his tales and history of the world of Middle-earth, where he took the centre of what makes a good story from the real historical events of Christ's birth, life, death then resurrection, which he saw as a happy ending after the suffering of death.

We speak of the "darkness before dawn" to express harrowing experiences that are followed by something good, yet Tolkien explored an idea which touched human hopes and fears even deeper. In this idea, there is crisis and apparent catastrophe with no sense of a happy outcome; then occurs a sudden, unexpected turn of events that is shockingly good. This is why he wrote of the consolation of this kind of happy ending, coining the term "eucatastrophe" to describe it. He argued that the term, translating as a "good" catastrophe, is the highest achievement of a "fairy tale" – his title for a story that creates another world where elves and similar magical creatures exist (that is, in the realm of fantasy). The other world might be on the borders of the story, or at the very heart of it. Although people can invent such stories, it is possible for events to take place in actual history that have all the qualities of a fairy tale or other imaginative stories with an element of fantasy, including the eucatastrophe.

Tolkien's word has now been added to the *Oxford English Dictionary*, which defines a *eucatastrophe* as follows: "Especially in a fictional narrative: a (sudden or unexpected) favourable turn of events; especially a resolution of this type; a happy ending." The dictionary also quotes from a letter Tolkien's own definition, as follows: "the sudden happy turn in a story which pierces you with a joy that brings tears".

In his famous essay "On Fairy-Stories", Tolkien links the consolation offered by a eucatastrophe with the Christian gospel, where there occurs in its first-century history two events he identifies as eucatastrophic. In his words: "The Birth of Christ is the eucatastrophe of Man's history. The Resurrection is the eucatastrophe of the story of the Incarnation."[5] Thus, human history tells a story in which the creator of all appears, taking on human flesh at the incarnation, which is the first sudden turn in the story. The later, otherwise tragic story of Christ's violent, unjust death also has a sudden, unexpected turn in the form of his return to physical life.

When Tolkien was recognizing the reality and importance of the sudden, happy turn – the eucatastrophe – he was acknowledging that he was featuring such in his fiction. The recognition brought together the heart of his imaginative creations and his Christian beliefs because both, as he saw it, pointed to a single truth. Like C.S. Lewis and Charles Williams, Sayers had an affinity with Tolkien and this famous view though, unlike them, she had never met him.

* * * * *

Revd James Welch, Director of Religious Broadcasting at the BBC, played a vital part in a period of the life and work of both C.S. Lewis and Sayers, going back to 1940 in the case of the latter, and to 1941 with the former. He was the person most responsible for the two of them becoming among the most well-known writers to be broadcast on wartime BBC Radio. Lewis popularized and effectively communicated basic Christian belief and Sayer's made the Gospel accounts of the life of Jesus Christ accessible and realistically acted, using familiar and common English (just as the original first-century Gospel writers used everyday language, that is common-or-garden international Greek, with some Aramaic thrown in). With the gradual restoration of a television service after the war years, BBC dramatizations of Sayers' Lord Peter Wimsey novels would eventually become normal household viewing. However, it was the series of radio plays, *The Man Born to Be King*, written by Sayers, that was to grip millions in the wartime audience, and which would shake up and at first outrage large numbers in the churches and the middle-classes.

Lewis' choice of title for his broadcast talks when they were published in one volume was *Mere Christianity*; it is true to say that the title "mere Christian" could apply as easily to Sayers, the high church Anglican, as it could to Lewis himself. He may have found the phrase in a church history by the Puritan Richard Baxter in the seventeenth century:

> I am a CHRISTIAN, a MEER CHRISTIAN, of
> no other Religion; and the Church that I am of
> is the Christian Church, and hath been visible
> where ever the Christian Religion and Church
> hath been visible: But must you know what

> Sect or Party I am of? I am against all Sects
> and dividing Parties: But if any will call Meer
> Christians by the name of a Party, because
> they take up with Meer Christianity, Creed,
> and Scripture, and will not be of any dividing
> or contentious Sect, I am of that Party which
> is so against Parties: If the Name CHRISTIAN
> be not enough, call me a CATHOLICK
> CHRISTIAN; not as that word signifieth an
> hereticating majority of Bishops, but as it
> signifieth one that hath no Religion, but that
> which by Christ and the Apostles was left to
> the Catholick Church, or the Body of Jesus
> Christ on Earth.[6]

Lewis and Sayers turned out to have a great affinity; thanks to Welch, both were well spotted by the BBC as communicators that were needed in the unusual circumstances of war. One of the many affinities, as an example, was their letter-writing. The three large volumes of Lewis' published letters make the quality and variety of his letters evident. Dorothy Sayers was also a prolific letter-writer, with over 3,000 of her letters published. Lewis was to describe her as "the first person of importance" who had ever sent him fan-mail. He in turn was to become a fan of hers. After receiving many letters from Sayers he commented: "Although you have so little time to write letters you are one of the great English letter writers."[7]

Lewis and Sayers were slowly to get acquainted with each other from her first letter to him, asking him to write on the subject of love and marriage for a planned series of books on wide-ranging contemporary issues to be called *Bridgeheads*. He declined, then soon after he invited her to lunch with him in Oxford, which would become a familiar request. In the correspondence over some years, letters began with "Dear Dr Lewis" or "Dear Miss Sayers", before finally becoming "Dear Jack" or "Dear Dorothy" as their friendship deepened. Given that she lived in Essex and London, she visited him fairly often in Oxford as their friendship developed.

Lewis and Sayers found themselves encouraging each other to create: Sayers suggested to him the urgent need to write an up-to-date and relevant book about the stumbling-block of miracles, a suggestion that was highly successful, with the appearance in 1947 of his book, *Miracles*. They didn't always get it right, as when she had wanted Lewis to write on love and marriage (having admired his science-fiction story, *The Hideous Strength,* centred as it was on the marriage of Mark and Jane Studdock, and comments in *The Screwtape Letters* most likely in Letter XIX[8]). Lewis unsuccessfully wished for Sayers to write something against the idea of women priests. He publicly praised Sayers' theologically astonishing *The Mind of the Maker,* which included bringing his praise into his discussion of miracles in his book of that name that Sayers had encouraged him to write.

> How a miracle can be no inconsistency,
> but the highest consistency, will be clear to
> those who have read Miss Dorothy Sayers'
> indispensable book, *The Mind of the Maker*.
> Miss Sayers' thesis is based on the analogy
> between God's relation to the world, on the
> one hand, and an author's relation to his book
> on the other.[9]

Lewis often praised the published book of her BBC Radio series, *The Man Born to Be King*. After Sayers sent him a copy he reread it annually for Lent, a custom which was only broken by his death six years after that of Sayers. In Revd Sherwood E. Wirt's interview with him weeks before his death in 1963, Lewis was asked, "What Christian writers have helped you?" His response was, "The contemporary book that has helped me the most is Chesterton's *The Everlasting Man*. Others are Edwin Bevan's book *Symbolism and Belief*, and Rudolf Otto's *The Idea of the Holy*, and the plays of Dorothy Sayers."[10]

Revd James Welch of the BBC gave strong support, with the backing of the rapidly expanding organization in wartime, to both Sayers and Lewis in their ventures into the mysterious world of broadcasting. The mysteries were made more complex by various departments having to move out of London to various places in England because of the grim realities of Nazi bombing and the real threat of invasion.

Lewis found his briefing from the BBC straightforward for his usually live fifteen-minute broadcasts from London. At Oxford his university lectures were frequent (and highly popular with the students), and he normally extemporized with the barest of notes using his phenomenal memory. He could easily handle the discipline of keeping to time with the short talks, for which he would produce a manuscript, as was the BBC way. Sayers' briefings however were far from simple in handling a radio play, which in wartime conditions had only brief rehearsals, or none at all in the case of the Sunday programme *Children's Hour* at that time. Fortunately, James Welch had a clear idea of what was needed for all aspects of the work and its wartime audience. He and Sayers saw eye to eye, as did Welch with Lewis. He was able to cope with a catastrophe which would have brought an end to *The Man Born to Be King* appearing on BBC Radio.

There are several accounts from people who worked with the BBC, recounting the history of the difficulties that Sayers had to confront as a professional writer, and not least the difficulties presented by wartime.[11] *The Man Born to Be King* was first commissioned by the BBC's *Children's Hour*. It was seen as following on nicely from the very successful, *He That Should Come,* a play which had been broadcast on Christmas Day 1938, and which focused upon the Nativity, and set in the hubbub of a crowded Bethlehem inn. The production, by Val Gielgud, brother of the famous actor Sir John Gielgud, worked perfectly. It pioneered all the realism she would later intend to have in *The Man Born to Be King.* Justin Phillips points out, "Drama came of age under the inspired leadership of Val Gielgud. Although he was not a Christian believer himself but firmly agnostic, Gielgud was responsible for propelling religious drama into a new era."[12]

Reviewing that 1938 BBC production, *The Times* was full of praise. Describing it as "a beautiful modern Nativity play", the review concluded:

> ...when Mary and Joseph come to the inn it
> all seems the most natural thing in the world
> that they should be grateful for a corner of the
> stable in which to sleep and that the Christ-
> child should be laid in a Manger. Miss Sayers
> has written a play which must have brought
> the Christmas story vividly before thousands
> of listeners.[13]

At first, all had seemed to go well – the BBC accepting Sayers' request that the series of plays should be aimed at older children, rather than at seven- to fourteen-year-olds, so that the mysteries in the stories could be retained. There was an almighty clash, however, between Sayers and an assistant director in the BBC's Children's Department, who felt her own professional standing and her committee's perspective should override the writer's views, no matter how distinguished. The climax was Sayers having to cancel her contract with the BBC as a matter of integrity about the value of artistic creativity over committee thinking. The envelope containing her cancellation letter also was full of the torn-up fragments of the contract. The angry Sayers was however settled by the peace-making and ever resourceful James Welch. He switched the production from the Children's Department to the Drama Department, under the directing of Val Gielgud. The result would be one of the highpoints in the history of BBC broadcasting.

The battle was not yet over, however. Although the legal prohibition of representing any person of the Godhead on stage did not apply to radio drama, it did not mean that the series could simply go ahead. Consequently, the BBC arranged a press conference on 15 December 1941 at Berners Hotel so Sayers could explain some of the challenges for a dramatist recounting the story of Jesus in contemporary discourse, which attracted the press. The statement she prepared and read from emphasized the importance of putting over Christ's incarnation as being believable as well as vivid. She pointed out why she was using modern English, and defended using an actor to impersonate Jesus. All was well until the press in attendance requested that Sayers read an example excerpt from its dialogue. The racy portion the honest Sayers read featured Matthew, the tax collector, and Andrew taking Philip to task as a sucker for allowing himself to be cheated by some dodgy fellows of a few drachmas.

The press immediately realized they had a big story. The *Daily Mail* was quick with its attention-grabbing headline: "BBC 'LIFE OF CHRIST' PLAY IN U.S. SLANG". With similar news stories abounding, condemnation was quick and furious. The BBC venture was condemned with terms such as "vulgar", "blasphemous" and "irreverent". A huge fund paid for a joint anti-campaign set up by the Protestant Truth Society and the Lord's Day Observance Society. James Welch also responded quickly – and strategically. A veteran foreign missionary before joining the BBC, Welch was determined to save a remarkable media event he knew would be a great help to BBC listeners in wartime, some of whom were nightly vulnerable to the reality of constant enemy bombing. Welch commented on the negative barrage from Fleet Street, and some religious groups that should have known better, and should have encouraged not condemned the evangelistic enterprise. The fact was that there were religious groups who, in their intolerance, had not read or heard the BBC plays on the life of Christ and who, unlike *The Times,* were indifferent to, or ignorant of, the powerful 1938 Christmas broadcast of Sayers' *He That Should Come,* which had engaged a huge audience throughout the country.

Welch's action in response was to send scripts to higher authorities. According to Justin Phillips, his support for Sayers and her play:

> ...was resolute and the hard treatment that Sayers and the BBC were receiving from the popular press enraged him. But, being the consummate politician that every head of religious broadcasting is required to be, he took the only action any senior BBC manager under fire would take. He referred it up. Scripts were sent to the CRAC, the Central Religious Advisory Committee, which comprised an Anglican bishop, dean and vicar, a Baptist, a Congregationalist, a Methodist, a Presbyterian and a Roman Catholic – all advisors to the BBC and representatives of the main Christian Churches in Britain. If they came down against the plays, if would have been the equivalent of "pistols at dawn" for Welch.

> The comments from the committee members poured
> in by post, telegram and telephone.[14]

From the overwhelmingly positive and enthusiastic response from the "official leaders and representatives of the Churches" the BBC decided they could broadcast *The Man Born to Be King*, and the rest is history. One result, as mentioned earlier, was that the Archbishop of Canterbury, William Temple, offered Sayers an honorary Lambeth doctorate in divinity for her creation of the BBC play series and her outstanding theological work, *The Mind of the Maker,* an offer which she declined. Her work was much wider than being for a Christian readership or audience, and she wished, with her well-known name, her private life not to be scrutinized.

After the series broadcast of *The Man Born to Be King* was complete, Val Gielgud reflected:

> It is not too much to claim that the plays,
> none of which called for a cast of less than
> forty, all of which were rehearsed and put
> on the air within forty-eight hours, set up
> a milestone of significant achievement for
> the radio play of which the value can hardly
> be estimated.... The majority of doubting
> Thomases was convinced. A medium which
> had not failed this greatest of subjects could
> no longer be neglected or thrust aside as
> unimportant.[15]

As a dedicated translator, knowledgeable of New Testament Greek, among other languages, Sayers was able to use her own translation of extracts from the four Gospels in her narrative of the life of Christ.[16] With great skill, she organized the drama into twelve parts, from the birth of Christ to the denouement (the eucatastrophe, to use Tolkien's term) of his resurrection.

As the original broadcasts were written and aired from 21 December 1941 to 18 October 1942, the twelve-part drama became embedded in Sayers' life. When studying a well-known contemporary book called *Who Moved the Stone?* by Frank Morison, she worked on the trial of Jesus, using the thorough book in her research. She was later amused to discover that its author was the person who managed the printing department at Benson's Advertising Agency while she had worked there, and later he became a director. His name was in fact Albert Ross (Frank Morison being a pen name, used for other books as well). She discovered this in 1946 when Ross contacted her by letter, to which she warmly responded in a letter.[17]

* * * * *

Sayers' friends from college days, those of the Mutual Admiration Society, had generally kept in touch with her and each other over the years, some of them more than others.[18] In their various ways, they were very conscious of the social changes leading toward another war, and their responsibility to do what they could within their particular powers. They took on board Sayers' preoccupation with creating and producing plays, and writing essays and books for the current climate – so different from her previous deep involvement with detection novels (though she remained president of the Detection Club until her sudden death). Muriel St Clare Byrne, with the help of her companion Marjorie Barber, were particularly involved in preparing the new book series, *Bridgeheads*, initiated by Sayers. They were joined by a later but important friend to Sayers, Helen Simpson, an Australian, who may have met her at the London home of Muriel and "Bar" (Marjorie). Simpson, a very active novelist and playwright, member of the Detection Club, and politician in the Liberal Party, was a stimulating friend to Sayers, and shared her faith. Her novel *Under Capricorn* was filmed and directed by Alfred Hitchcock, and she contributed to the Detection Club round robins, *The Floating Admiral* in 1931 and to *Ask a Policeman* in 1933. To the distress of her friends, Helen Simpson was to die from cancer after months of suffering in 1940 at the age of forty-two. Along with Muriel and "Bar", the novel of *Busman's Honeymoon* had been dedicated to her. Various books for the *Bridgeheads* series had been enthusiastically suggested by the friends, but ultimately only Sayers' groundbreaking book, *The Mind of the Maker*, and Una Ellis-Fermor's *Masters of Reality*, made publication for the series,[19] and some others were published elsewhere. (Una Ellis-Fermor studied at Somerville College around the same time as Sayers.[19]) Those directly involved, under Sayers' influence, described the thinking behind the hoped-for series:

> A real value for life must be such as to satisfy
> man's nature as a whole. No value for life is
> real that involves the denial of any part of
> human personality…. We shall try to quicken
> the creative spirit which enables man to
> build systems in the light of his spiritual,
> intellectual, and social needs. We aim at the
> Resurrection of Faith, the Revival of Learning
> and the Re-integration of Society.[20]

During this time Muriel St Clare Byrne was perhaps more aware than others of the difficulties between Sayers and her husband Mac, yet he was not entirely separate from the affections of the group. Mo Moulton, in her group biography, *Mutual Admiration Society*, records how Charis Frankenberg's daughter, Ursula, was welcomed to Sayers' and Mac's home in Witham while studying at the Essex Institute of Agriculture. When Ursula asked her mother why she had lost contact with a pleasant woman like Sayers, she responded apologetically to her old friend, and contact was renewed.[21]

* * * * *

After Mac was suddenly taken by a stroke on 9 June 1950, one of the many ways his death impacted Sayers was for her to be able to spend much more time in London. Her comfortable flat in Bloomsbury was hence much more in use. This helped her connections with her friends like Muriel and "Bar", the Detection Club, and also her involvement with St Anne's House, in Dean Street, Soho. St Anne's Anglican church had been wrecked during the war by a landmine, but for its surviving clock tower and the parish house. The base of the church tower was adapted into a small church area. Sayers had been attracted for a long time by St Anne's visionary priest, Father Patrick McLaughlin. After the war damage, he and others wished for the surviving buildings to be a place where intellectuals with questions could experience well thought-out debate about Christian faith. The rewarding outcome was the establishment of "St Anne's House, a Centre of Cultural Studies". Sayers would be deeply committed to working with it for the years left of her life. There had also been some exploration of the idea of launching a London-based Socratic Club, following the successful Socratic Club at Oxford University, which would be chaired by Sayers. She had spoken at the club in Oxford, and her friend C.S. Lewis had become heavily involved in it thanks to the efforts of poet and church-based student worker, Stella Aldwinkle. The London Socratic Club however failed to materialize but St Anne's House was viable. James Brabazon,

Sayers' future biographer, was present at the first St Anne's course set up there in the summer of 1943, entitled, "Christian Faith and Contemporary Culture", attending a lecture by Sayers on drama. Other lectures on that promising very first course included, he tells us, T.S. Eliot on literature, BBC's Revd James Welch on broadcasting, and other professionals on journalism, and on the visual arts.

* * * * *

For a number of years Sayers' preoccupation with the reality of evil, the burden of sin, and the presence of war both physical and spiritual, developed. Her dramas, *The Zeal of Thy House* and *The Devil to Pay* and other plays, showed her work was on a trajectory toward redemption, hope, and the happy ending following catastrophe – whether catastrophe of war or the suffering of affliction. In this trajectory the BBC had already played an important part, as would a new imprint, Penguin Classics. Also to play an important and connected role was a friendship that had developed with Charles Williams from the early 1930s, and which intensified in his final years during the Second World War. Connected with Charles Williams and Penguin Classics, and taking shape in the wartime and post-war years, was a love for one of the greatest medieval poets, Dante Alighieri, creator of *La Commedia* (*The Divine Comedy*), whom she found dramatically relevant to her developing concerns, and to a war-torn world attempting to reconstruct. She found the happy ending in his masterpiece (indicated in its title), as she translated and annotated it, and earlier a happy ending in what she believed was the greatest story ever told, and which she retold as *The Man Born to Be King*. In the radio drama, and in the epic translation of Dante's great poem, her fame was preserved, as was her fame from the Golden Age of detection fiction. At the heart of her achievement is a theological understanding of *The Divine Comedy* and its author.[22]

Sayers came across a review of a new book by Williams in the *Sunday Times* during August 1943 called *The Figure of Beatrice*. She obtained a copy of the book simply because it was by Williams, whom she greatly admired, and whose company she enjoyed. There is no doubt about this. After his death, she reflected that while C.S. Lewis was a very disciplined and talented writer, Williams was very original and profound, marked by genuine genius. Sayers thoroughly endorsed his overall emphasis in his works on images in poetry and other literature, such as in Dante, and likely also his responses to biblical images. His book took her into the mind and soul of Dante, and the depths of his image (or "figure") of Beatrice, whom Dante had encountered in thirteenth-century Florence. In his love for her, he had to suffer and live with her early death. The impact Williams had upon Sayers may also be seen in her modern miracle-play, *The Just Vengeance*, especially written for production in Lichfield Cathedral in 1946. It was also inspired by a passage from *Paradise*, the third volume of *The Divine Comedy*. Its story setting in wartime Lichfield evokes Williams' affirmation of the image of the city. In addition its characterization of an airman at the moment of death, at which the entire action of the play takes place, is suggestive also of Williams' writings.

Sayers' home town of Witham rarely experienced enemy bombing, unlike many large English cities. However, air raid warnings did sound there, and she like her neighbours would make their way quickly to shelters. One had been built at the back of her house. One night during August 1944, as the siren sounded, Sayers grabbed a book she was planning to enjoy sometime, in order to read in the shelter. It was her mother's copy of Dante's *Inferno* (aka, *Hell*), the first of the three volumes of *The Divine Comedy*. It had the original old Italian set side-by-side with an English translation.

Some time later she wrote down her overwhelming response to reading Dante. Sayers noted she had come across nothing at all like its impact since she first encountered Dumas' *The Three Musketeers* when thirteen. She devoured her meals as quickly as possible, neglected much, such as her letter-writing and her work, and missed sleep. Reading Dante even made her fail to notice the distinctive sound of a doodlebug, whose sudden silence would signify the flying bomb overhead was now falling to earth.[23]

She had written to Charles Williams a number of times in the past, but her new absorption in Dante's epic set off a deluge of her letters to him – one was thirty pages long, in her small handwriting – letters which carried her excited but inspired responses to what she was reading. In the process, the gifted linguist was quickly mastering old Italian, helped no doubt by her knowledge of Latin. Most of all, she realized that Dante was an eminent storyteller, master of narrative in his verse. Her friend "Bar" once said something striking to her, after her own discovery of Dante. She said that it was nothing like what she anticipated: dignified and solemn, along the lines of Milton's *Paradise Lost*. Rather, she thought it like someone comfortable in an armchair, telling a story to you.[24] Sayers own response had been that no other storyteller could be compared with him. Though Williams' letters of reply were usually much shorter than Sayers', they were full of encouragement.

Translating *The Divine Comedy*, and adding a wealth of annotations took up much of the final years of Sayers' life. It was a period of great fulfillment for her; already in the past she had delighted in translating, such as *Tristan in Brittany*[25] (the story of Tristan and Iseult), and Gospel passages in *The Man Born to Be King*. She began her work for Penguin Classics at the request of then series editor, E.V. Rieu (who himself translated several classics such as the *Odyssey* and *The Four Gospels*). From then until 1957 Sayers was working on the *Divine Comedy* trilogy, with an interruption in 1956 to translate a favourite, *The Song of Roland,* also for the Penguin series. Had she continued without that break it is likely that she would have completed the Dante translation. As it was, when she had completed translating Canto XX, two thirds of her way through the third volume, *Paradise,* with its images of heaven, death interrupted her work. Canto XX ends thus:

> Così da quella imagine divina,
> per farmi chiara la mia corta vista,
> data mi fu soave medicina.

> E come a buon cantor buon citarista
> fa seguitar lo guizzo de la corda,
> in che più di piacer lo canto acquista,

> sì, mentre ch'e' parlò, sì mi ricorda
> ch'io vidi le due luci benedette,
> pur come batter d'occhi si concorda,

> con le parole mover le fiammette.

The last canto Sayers completed before her death reveals how, experiencing the visions of Paradise, Dante's mind is being cleared. In Paradise Dante has learned much from his guide, Beatrice. The canto explains that his mind has just been clarified some more by his vision of a mystic eagle. The concluding lines speak of the illumination of this celestial image of the eagle healing like medicine the short-sightedness of his mind. The poem continues in the next canto, untranslated by Sayers, with Dante now ready to ascend with Beatrice to the Seventh Heaven of Saturn, with its great golden ladder running higher into Paradise.

Providentially, there was her close friend and goddaughter Barbara Reynolds, an excellent Dante scholar and writer, who would take over the large task of completing the translation, and adding the introduction, notes and commentaries. Therefore, the final volume of *The Divine Comedy* for Penguin Classics was able to be published five years later. She wrote in the foreword:

> In completing this translation of the *Paradiso*
> I have done my best to continue in the style
> of the first twenty cantos. My hope that I
> may have, to some degree, succeeded rests
> on the fact that over a period of eleven years,
> and particularly during the last three years
> of her life, I was in contact with Dorothy
> Sayers with regard to her work on Dante. In
> conversations and in letters she discussed in
> detail her methods of translation, the reasons
> for her choice of diction, her preferences as
> to style and rhythm; sometimes she sent as
> many as ten or twelve trial renderings of a
> single passage, and frequently she wrote long
> letters almost wholly concerned with the
> technique of verse translation. When I learned,
> after her death, that she had expressed the
> wish that I should continue her work, I found
> that I had accumulated a store of information,
> almost of instruction, as to how to proceed.[26]

EPILOGUE

"Let us thank the Author who invented her."
C.S. Lewis[1]

It was a few days before Christmas 1957. After the sudden death of his mother, Anthony Fleming had travelled to Sunnyside Cottage in Witham. Muriel St Clare Byrne opened the front door to the young man, who informed her he was Dorothy Sayers' son. She wrapped him in her arms and we are told that she said, "Thank God you've come."[2] This was the first Sayers' close friend knew of his existence. Byrne had never met Bill White, so she did not see how much Anthony physically resembled his father. In among her shock and grief, she had steadied herself for the appointed task of being Sayers' literary executrix, along with Anthony as executor. Sayers had in fact told her son that Lloyds Bank were the executors. Lloyds had no knowledge of this being the case, and had no trace of a will. Therefore, the role went to Anthony and Byrne. At Witham, the will also presented a problem: it was missing. Sayers' secretary looked high and low for it, without success.

Byrne, however, quickly found it in an empty drawer of her friend's familiar tallboy, underneath its lining, where Sayers had hidden it long ago. The will bore a date of eighteen years before.

Dorothy Sayers' ashes were deposited at St Anne's House, Soho within a refurbished ground floor of the church tower, where later a memorial plaque was placed by The Dorothy L. Sayers Society.

Michael Gilbert was a member of the Detection Club, and that is how he had known Sayers. He wrote that "just before Christmas in 1957 my wife and I were up in London buying Christmas cards and met Dorothy on the same errand. Two days later we got a card from her. This didn't normally happen, but perhaps seeing us put her in mind of it. It was a macabre thing to receive. The *Evening Standard* had announced her death on the previous day."[3]

While Christmas shopping in central London, Sayers had also viewed a new portrait of herself by Sir William Hutchison for the year's Exhibition of the Royal Society of Portrait Painters at the Royal Institute Galleries at Piccadilly. Soon after her arrival at Sunnyside Cottage in Witham that very evening she was suddenly to die of a stroke. Her body was discovered in her house by the cleaner first thing the next morning.

After Christmas, on 15 January, in Saint Margaret's Church at Westminster, a crowd of her friends joined together at her memorial service.

Muriel St Clare Byrne and Anthony Fleming thoroughly looked after her estate. Sayers had declared that she did not wish for her biography to be written, if ever, until fifty years after her death. Behind this wish was her long-standing feeling of wariness over what would be revealed of her past. She was firmly aware of her failings, and she carried her strong sense of sin, which she believed was a central key in life as to why in human history the world constantly goes wrong. When the first biography of Sayers was published in 1975,[4] and revealed that she'd had a child out of wedlock, her trustees decided it was then necessary to commission an authorized biography, despite her aversion to publicity of her privacy. This appeared in 1981, written by James Brabazon, who had known her, and had access to materials not then available to others, such as Sayers' prolific correspondence.

Dorothy L. Sayers: A chronology

1713   Great sluice burst at Denver in the Fens (inspiration for the flood in Sayers' *The Nine Tailors*).

1854   Birth of Henry Sayers, Tittleshall, Norfolk. Son of Revd Robert Sayers.

1879   Opening of Somerville Hall (later renamed Somerville College), Oxford.
Henry Sayers obtains a degree in Divinity from Magdalen College, Oxford.

1880   Henry Sayers ordained as minister of the Church of England in Hereford.

1884   Henry Sayers becomes headmaster of the Christ Church Choir School.

1892   Henry Sayers and Helen Mary ("Nell/Nelly") Leigh marry.

1893   Dorothy Leigh Sayers born on 13 June, in the old Choir House at 1, Brewer Street, Oxford. Christened by Henry Sayers, 15 July, over the road in Christ Church Cathedral.

1894   BA qualifications opened to women in England, but without the award of a university BA degree.

1897   Henry Sayers accepted the living of Bluntisham-cum-Earith in East Anglia as rector.

1906   Dorothy discovers Alexander Dumas' influential *The Three Musketeers* at the age of thirteen.

1908   On approaching her sixteenth birthday, Dorothy's parents decided to send her to boarding school. Dorothy is taken to see Shakespeare's *Henry V* in London.

1909   Sent to the Godolphin School in Salisbury, 17 January, as a boarder.

1910   Dorothy pressured into being confirmed as an Anglican at Salisbury Cathedral.

1911   Dorothy comes first in the country in the Cambridge Higher Local Examinations, gaining distinctions in French and Spoken German.
Nearly dies from the consequences of measles; sent home to recover.

1912   Kept at home for final term for fear of a "scarlet fever scare" at the school.
Wins a significant Gilchrist scholarship to Somerville College, Oxford.
Goes up to the college in October.

1914   Summer trip to the Continent which becomes dangerous; hastily returning as First World War begins.

1915   Gains a first-class award in modern (medieval) French, but as a woman does not qualify for receiving a degree.
Begins reading detective fiction.

1916   Makes an attempt at teaching French in Hull, in the autumn term.
Op. I published – a small volume of poems published by Blackwell's of Oxford.

1917   Leaves school teaching; begins an editing post in Oxford as an intern at Blackwell's Publishers, under Basil Blackwell, and funded by her father.

1918   Eric Whelpton in Oxford.
Captain "Mac" Fleming leaves the army with the war over.
Women over thirty receive vote in Britain.

Sayers' *Catholic Tales and Christian Songs,* a second book of verse, is published.

1919   Fleming's book, *How to See the Battlefields* is published. He becomes a Fleet Street journalist and photographer.

Sayers leaves Blackwell's.

Goes to France to work with Eric Whelpton in Ecole des Roches in Normandy.

1920   Sayers returns to England in September.

Teaches temporarily in London; tries her hand at detective stories, with the sudden emergence of Lord Peter Wimsey.

Receives University of Oxford BA and MA in Modern Languages – among one of first groups of women to receive them.

1921   Meets Russian American writer and translator John Cournos; falls in love with him.

Finishes her first Peter Wimsey novel *Whose Body?* with no publisher as yet.

Moves into a flat at 24, Great James Street, in the Bloomsbury area of London.

1922   Gets a literary agent, almost certainly with the help of John Cournos.

Begins at S.H. Benson's Advertising Agency in Kingsway as a copywriter and "ideas man".

Starts writing *Clouds of Witness.*

Whose Body? is taken by a US publisher via her agent.

Relationship with Cournos ends; he moves to US.

Sayers meets Bill White.

1923   *Whose Body?* published in US and then later in UK.
Accidentally conceives in April; father is Bill White.
Takes a carefully planned brief leave of absence from
Benson's in November.

1924   Gives birth in secrecy to her son, John Anthony, on
3 January.
Hastily arranges for her older cousin Ivy Shrimpton
to foster him.
In April, ends relationship with Bill White, learning
he is married.
Discovers Cournos has married a crime writer in US,
Sybil Norton.

1925   "Mac" Fleming's divorce becomes final and he
courts Sayers.

1926   *Cloud of Witnesses* published.
Marries Oswald "Mac" Atherton Fleming, 13 April.
Fleming joins Sayers in her small London flat at 24,
Great James Street.

1927   *Unnatural Death* published (*The Dawson Pedigree* in
US).

1928   Henry Sayers dies suddenly.
Sayers' mother, and her elderly sister Mabel, move to
Witham, Essex; Sayers and Mac keep on the London
flat.
Edits the first series of *Great Short Stories of Detection,
Mystery, and Horror* (Gollancz), called *The Omnibus of
Crime* in US.
The Unpleasantness at the Bellona Club, and *Lord Peter
Views the Body* published. The Detection Club starts
to form.

1929   Sayers' mother dies.
        Tristan in Brittany published.
        Acquires a new London agent, David Higham.
        Leaves employment at Benson's to focus on writing.
1930   Prepares for a BBC Radio series, *The Scoop*, along
        with the Detection Club.
        The Documents in the Case, with coauthor, Robert
        Eustace, published.
        Sayers and Mac holiday in Galloway.
        Strong Poison published: introduces Lord Peter's love
        interest, Harriet Vane.
1931   *Five Red Herrings* published (*Suspicious Characters* in
        US).
        Researches campanology for a new mystery novel.
        The Floating Admiral published (with Detection
        Club members, including G. K. Chesterton, Agatha
        Christie, and Ronald Knox) as well as *The Scoop*
        written jointly by members of the Detection Club,
        including Agatha Christie and E.C. Bentley.
1932   Works on *My Edwardian Childhood*, never finished.
        Have His Carcase published.
1933   *Murder Must Advertise* and *Hangman's Holiday*
        published.
        Decisions about marriage and son are made during
        brief motoring holiday with Muriel St Clare Byrne.
1934   *The Nine Tailors* published.
        Attends a Somerville Gaudy (a reunion for its
        alumni).
        Sayers and Mac informally adopt Anthony in
        December, aged 10.
        Anthony remains in the care of Ivy Shrimpton.
1935   Sayers completes *Busman's Honeymoon* playscript
        with Muriel St Clare Byrne. *Gaudy Night* published.

1936   Works on *Thrones, Dominations* (completed
        posthumously by Jill Paton Walsh).
        Completes book adaptation of *Busman's Honeymoon*.
        Play of *Busman's Honeymoon* opens in the West End of
        London, runs for nine months.
        Privately prints *Papers Relating to the Family of Wimsey*.
1936   Hires first secretary.
        Charles Williams persuades the Canterbury Festival to
        commission a play from her.
1937   Play and novel, *Busman's Honeymoon* published.
        Completes *The Zeal of Thy House* and presents the play
        at Canterbury.
        Visits Venice with close friend Marjorie Barber.
1938   Sayers researches material for a biography of Wilkie
        Collins (never completed).
        Manages a tour of *The Zeal of Thy House*.
        Anthony Fleming starts boarding school at Malvern
        College.
        Val Gielgud produces *He That Should Come* for BBC
        Radio's *Children's Hour* at Christmas, on the Nativity.
1939   *The Devil to Pay* (on Faustus) is performed at the
        Canterbury Festival; published in June.
        In the Teeth of the Evidence and Other Stories published.
1940   Receives proposal from Revd Dr James W. Welch,
        Director of Religious Broadcasting BBC, for a series on
        the life of Christ.
        Starts the *Bridgeheads* series (*The Mind of the Maker* to
        be its first publication).
        Love All is performed in London.
        Begins radio scripts for installments of a major BBC
        project, *The Man Born to Be King*.
        Begin Here is published.

Starts working on a new passion, the poetry of
Dante Alighieri, with strong encouragement from
Charles Williams.

1941   Val Gielgud agrees to produce *The Man Born to Be
King* for the BBC. It is broadcast from 21 December
1941 to 18 October 1942.

Sayers connects with Father Patrick McLaughlin at St
Anne's Church, Soho, in his concern to reach out to
"thinking Pagans".

The Mind of the Maker published.

1942   Anthony Fleming wins a history scholarship to
Balliol College, Oxford.

Sayers writes to C.S. Lewis suggesting he writes for
her new *Bridgehead*s series; their first known meeting
takes place over lunch.

1943   *The Man Born to Be King* published; numerous
reprints during wartime economy printing and after.

Reluctantly refuses a doctorate of divinity offered by
the Archbishop of Canterbury.

1944   In Chichester with T.S. Eliot at a September
conference on religion and the arts, along with
architects, painters, and sculptors.

Joins St Anne's House Advisory Council.

Begins translating Dante's *Inferno* (*Hell*).

Lichfield Cathedral commissions *The Just Vengeance*.

1945   Penguin Books offer a contract for translation of *The
Divine Comedy*.

Sayers contributes a chapter on Dante to *Essays
Presented to Charles Williams,* edited by C.S. Lewis.

1946   Lectures at the Oxford Summer School of Italian
Studies.

Anthony Fleming finds out that Sayers is his mother.

The Just Vengeance performed at Lichfield Festival.
Unpopular Opinions (with twenty-one essays)
published.
Meets scholar Barbara Reynolds, whom she
befriends.

1947   Mac suffers deterioration of health.
Essays Presented to Charles Williams published.

1948   *Four Sacred Plays* published.
Completes her translation of Dante's *Hell* (*Inferno*).
Anthony Fleming is awarded first-class honours
degree in PPE (Politics, Philosophy, and Economics)
at Balliol College, Oxford.
Sayers starts work on *The Emperor Constantine*
(for Colchester Cathedral Festival), and starts her
translation of *Purgatory*.

1949   *Creed or Chaos?*, a collection of seven of her essays,
published.
Penguin Classics publishes her translation of *Hell*
(*Inferno*).

1950   Mac Fleming is taken into hospital in April.
Sayers awarded Honorary Doctor of Letters by the
University of Durham in May.
Mac dies of a stroke on 9 June.

1951   Performance of *The Emperor Constantine* at
Colchester Festival, which is soon published.

1952   Appointed churchwarden at St Thomas's Church,
Regent Street, London. Serves for the remaining
years of her life.

1953   Involved in the restoration of St Thomas's Church.

1954   Kathleen Nott attacks Sayers and other Christian
apologists in her *The Emperor's Clothes*.
Sayers completes the translation of *Purgatory* from
The Divine Comedy.

1955   *Introductory Papers on Dante* published.
        Translation of Dante's *Purgatory* published.
        Temporarily puts aside her work on Dante's *Paradise*
        to translate the medieval *The Song of Roland*.

1957   Article, "Christian Belief about Heaven and Hell",
        appears in the *Sunday Times*.
        Becomes a godmother to her adult friend (and later,
        editor and biographer), Barbara Reynolds.
        Dies suddenly, Tuesday 17 December, just after
        returning home to Witham from a brief visit to
        London.

1962   Penguin Classics publishes *Paradise*, completed by
        Barbara Reynolds after death of Sayers.

1973   Sayers' short story, "Striding Folly", published in a
        book collection with "Tallboys" and "The Haunted
        Policeman".

1975   Janet Hitchman's *Such a Strange Lady,* published.
        This is the first biography of Sayers, and it revealed
        the secret that Sayers was the mother of Anthony
        Fleming.

1976   Formation of The Dorothy L. Sayers Society.

Appendix

Charles Williams' review of *The Nine Tailors* by Dorothy L. Sayers

"The new Sayers" is not merely admirable; it
is adorable. There were, in Miss Sayers's more
recent books, signs that a strange element
was struggling to be free. In one this element
seemed like philosophy; in one like fantasy.
It has now become perfectly freed itself,
and become perfectly united with her other
capacities. *The Nine Tailors* is consequently
not a tale of murder, but an experience of life.
There is a murder, and there is detection; there
is Lord Peter Wimsey. The surroundings are
the Fen country; church bells, with all the art
of their ringing; a vicar and the villagers; dykes,
and the breaking of dykes, and a flood.
Laughter and pity and terror, clarity and
mystery, inform all these things, and as Miss
Sayer's perfect mastery moves on to its climax
in the tower of the church where the refugees,
admirably ordered by a mortal and immortal
ritual, find shelter, the book becomes in itself
a kind of judgment. The powers of earth and
air denounce and encourage, and below them
lies the wide sweep of waters. There is nothing
supernatural – unless indeed we and our life
and all our art are supernatural, as some have

held. But it is the reflection of our dark and passionate life itself which those waters hold and those bells proclaim. It is a great book.

News Chronicle, 17, January 1934, p. 4.

Select Bibliography

Brabazon, James, *Dorothy L. Sayers: A Biography* (with a Preface by Anthony Fleming) (New York: Charles Scribner's Sons, 1981).

Brittain, Vera, *Chronicle of Youth: Great War Diary 1913–1917* (London: Collins Fontana, 1981, 1982).

Brittain, Vera, *Testament of Youth* (London: Victor Gollancz, 1933).

Brittain, Vera, *The Women at Oxford: A Fragment of History* (New York: The Macmillan Company, 1960).

Brunskill, Ian (ed.), "Dorothy L. Sayers," in *Great Lives: A Century in Obituaries* (London: Times Books, 2007).

Christie, Agatha, "Preface," in *Ask a Policeman* by members of the Detection Club, 80th Anniversary Edition (London: Harper, 2013).

Coomes, David, *Dorothy L. Sayers: A Careless Rage for Life* (Oxford: Lion Publishing, 1992).

Cournos, John, *Autobiography* (New York: Putnam, 1935).

Dale, Alzina Stone (ed.), *Dorothy L. Sayers: The Centenary Celebration* (New York: Walker and Company, 1993).

Dale, Alzina Stone, *Maker and Craftsman: The Story of Dorothy L. Sayers* (Grand Rapids, Michigan: Wm B. Eerdmans, 1978).

DuBose, Martha Hailey, *Women of Mystery: The Lives and Works of Notable Women Crime Novelists* (New York: Macmillan, 2000).

Duriez, Colin and Porter, David, *The Inklings Handbook: The Lives, Thought and Writings of C.S. Lewis, J.R.R. Tolkien, Charles Williams, Owen Barfield and Their Friends* (London: Azure, 2001).

Duriez, Colin, *J.R.R. Tolkien and C.S. Lewis: The Story of Their Friendship* (Stroud, Gloucestershire: Sutton Publishing, 2003).

Duriez, Colin, *C.S. Lewis: A Biography of Friendship* (Oxford: Lion Books, 2013).

Duriez, Colin, *The Oxford Inklings: Lewis, Tolkien, and Their Circle* (Oxford: Lion Hudson, 2015).

Eliot, T.S., *The Idea of a Christian Society and Other Writings* (London: Faber and Faber, 1939, second edition, 1982).

Elsby, Jon, *Light in the Darkness: Four Christian Apologists* (UK: CentreHouse Press, 2016).

Fleming, Capt. Atherton, *How to See the Battlefields* (New York: Funk and Wagnalls Company, 1919).

Frankenburg, Charis, *Not Old, Madam, Vintage* (Lavenham, Suffolk: Galaxy Press, 1975).

Gilbert, Colleen B., *A Bibliography of the Works of Dorothy L. Sayers* (Hamden, Connecticut: Archon Books, 1978).

Graham, Malcolm, *Oxford in the Great War* (Barnsley, S. Yorks: Pen and Sword Military, 2014).

Gyford, Janet, "Mike Wadhams and 'Cocksmiths' (22–26 Newland Street. Witham)", in *Essex Archaeology and History News*, no. 111, April 1991.

H.D., *Bid Me to Live* (London: Virago Modern Classics, 1984).

Hitchman, Janet, *"Such a Strange Lady"*: An Introduction to Dorothy L. Sayers (1893–1957) (London: NEL Paperback, New English Library, Paperback Edition, 1976).

Hollenberg, Donna Krolik (ed.), "Art and Ardor in World War One: Selected Letters from H.D. to John Cournos", in *The Iowa Review*, Volume 16, Issue 3 Fall: *H.D. Centennial Issue*, 1986.

Hone, Ralph E., *Dorothy L. Sayers: A Literary Biography* (Kent, Ohio: The Kent State University Press, 1979).

Hooper, Walter (ed.), *C.S. Lewis: Collected Letters, Vol. I* (London: HarperCollins, 2000).

Hooper, Walter (ed.), *C.S. Lewis: Collected Letters, Vol. II* (London: HarperCollins, 2004).

Hooper, Walter (ed.), *C.S. Lewis: Collected Letters, Vol. III* (London: HarperCollins, 2006).

James, P.D., *Talking About Detective Fiction* (Oxford and London: Bodleian Library and Faber and Faber, 2010).

Kenney, Catherine, *The Remarkable Case of Dorothy L. Sayers* (Kent, Ohio and London, England: The Kent State University Press, 1990).

Leigh, Margaret, *The Fruit in the Seed* (London: Phoenix House, 1952).

Leigh, Percival, *Comic Latin Grammar* (Fleet Street, London: Charles Tilt, 1840).

Leonardi, Susan J., *Dangerous by Degrees: Women at Oxford and the Somerville College Novelists* (New Brunswick, New Jersey, and London: Rutgers University Press, 1989).

Lewis, C.S. (ed.), *Essays Presented to Charles Williams* (London: Oxford University Press, 1947).

Lewis, C.S. *On Stories and Other Essays on Literature* (New York: A Harvest Book, Harcourt Inc., 1982).

Lewis, C.S., *Miracles* (London: Geoffrey Bles, 1947).

Lewis, C.S., *Surprised by Joy* (London: Geoffrey Bles, 1955).

Lewis, C.S., *The Allegory of Love* (Oxford: Clarendon Press, 1936).

Lindop, Grevel, *Charles Williams: The Third Inkling* (New York and London: Oxford University Press, 2015).

Loades, Ann, "Dorothy L. Sayers," in Lindsay Jones (ed.), *Encyclopedia of Religion* (Detroit, Michigan: Macmillan Reference, Vol. 12, second edition, 2005).

Loades, Ann, preface to Suzanne Bray (ed.), *Dorothy L. Sayers: The Christ of the Creeds & Other Broadcast Messages to the British People during World War II* (Hurstpierpoint, West Sussex: The Dorothy L. Sayers Society, 2008).

McGrath, Alister E., *The Intellectual World of C.S. Lewis* (Oxford: Wiley-Blackwell, 2014).

Moulton, Mo, *Mutual Admiration Society* (London: Corsair, 2019).

Norrington, A.L.P., *Blackwell's 1879–1979: The History of a Family Firm* (Oxford: Blackwell, 1983).

Percy, Sandra, *Dorothy L. Sayers: More Than a Crime Fiction Writer* (Self published, ISBN 145280169X, 2010).

Phillips, Justin, *C.S. Lewis at the BBC: Messages of Hope in the Darkness of War* (London: HarperCollins, 2002).

Reynolds, Barbara (ed.), *Dorothy L. Sayers: Child and Woman of her Time. Volume Five. A Supplement to The Letters of Dorothy L. Sayers* (Dorothy L. Sayers Society, Cambridge: Carole Green Publishing).

Reynolds, Barbara (ed.), *The Letters of Dorothy L. Sayers, Volume One (1899–1936: The making of a detective novelist)* (London: Hodder & Stoughton, 1995).

Reynolds, Barbara (ed.), *The Letters of Dorothy L. Sayers, Volume Two (1937–1943: From novelist to playwright)* (The Dorothy L. Sayers Society, Cambridge: Carole Green Publishing, 1997).

Reynolds, Barbara, (ed.), *The Letters of Dorothy L. Sayers, Volume Three (1944–1950: A Noble Daring)* (The Dorothy L. Sayers Society, Cambridge: Carole Green Publishing, 1998).

Reynolds, Barbara (ed.), *The Letters of Dorothy L. Sayers, Volume Four (1951–1957: In the midst of life)* (The Dorothy L. Sayers Society, Cambridge: Carole Green Publishing, 2000).

Reynolds, Barbara, "Search or Statement?" in *The Passionate Intellect: Dorothy L. Sayers' Encounter with Dante* (Eugene, Oregon: Wipf & Stork, 2005).

Reynolds, Barbara, *Dorothy L. Sayers: Her Life and Soul* (London: Hodder and Stoughton, 1993).

Reynolds, Barbara, *The Passionate Intellect: Dorothy L. Sayers' Encounter with Dante* (Oregon: Wipf and Stock Publishers, 2005).

Saintsbury, George, introduction in Dorothy L. Sayers (trans.), *Tristan in Brittany* (London: Ernest Benn, 1929).

Satterthwaite, Alfred, "John Cournos and 'H.D.,'" in *Twentieth Century Literature,* vol. 22, no. 4 (December 1976), pp. 394–410.

Sayers, Dorothy L. (ed.), *Great Short Stories of Detection, Mystery, and Horror,* vol. I (London: Victor Gollancz, 1928).

Sayers, Dorothy L. (ed.), *Great Short Stories of Detection, Mystery, and Horror*, vol. II (London: Victor Gollancz, 1931).

Sayers, Dorothy L. (ed.), *Great Short Stories of Detection, Mystery, and Horror,* vol. III (London: Victor Gollancz, 1934).

Sayers, Dorothy L., "Christian Belief about Heaven and Hell", in *The Great Mystery of Life Hereafter* (London: Hodder and Stoughton, 1957).

Sayers, Dorothy L., introduction in Dorothy L. Sayers (ed.), *Great Short Stories of Detection, Mystery, and Horror,* vol. I (London: Victor Gollancz, 1928).

Sayers, Dorothy L., "Is There A Definite Evil Power?" in Ronald Selby Wright (ed.), *Asking Them Questions: A Selection* (London: Oxford University Press, 1953).

Sayers, Dorothy L., preface to *The Devil to Pay* (London: Victor Gollancz, 1930).

Sayers, Dorothy L., "The Lost Tools of Learning"", in *The Poetry of Search and the Poetry of Statement* (London: Victor Gollancz, 1963).

Sayers, Dorothy L., *Gaudy Night* (London: Victor Gollancz. 1935).

Sayers, Dorothy L., *Op. 1.* (Oxford: B.H. Blackwell, 1916).

Sayers, Dorothy L., *The Man Born to Be King: A Play-Cycle on the Life of Our Lord and Saviour Jesus Christ* (London: Victor Gollancz, 1943).

Sayers, Dorothy L., *The Poetry of Search and the Poetry of Statement* (London: Victor Gollancz, 1963).

Sayers, Dorothy L., *Whose Body?* (New York: Boni and Liveright, 1923).

Shideler, Mary McDermott, *The Theology of Romantic Love: A Study in the Writings of Charles Williams* (Grand Rapids, Michigan: Eerdmans, 1966).

Sibley, Brian, *The Book of Guinness Advertising* (Enfield, Middlesex: Guinness Superlatives, 1985).

Simmons, Laura K., *Creed Without Chaos: Exploring Theology in the Writings of Dorothy L. Sayers* (Grand Rapids, Michigan: Baker Academic, 2005).

Symons, Julian, *Bloody Murder From the Detective Story to the Crime Novel: A History* (London: Faber and Faber, 1972).

Thurmer, John, *A Detection of the Trinity* (Exeter: The Paternoster Press, 1984).

Thurmer, John, *Reluctant Evangelist: Papers on the Christian Thought of Dorothy L. Sayers* (Hurstpierpoint, West Sussex: The Dorothy L. Sayers Society, 1996).

Trueman, A.E., *Geology and Scenery in England and Wales* (Harmondsworth, Middlesex: Penguin, revised edition, 1971), p 143.

Ward, Maisie, *Gilbert Keith Chesterton* (London: Sheed & Ward, 1944).

Welch, James, foreword in Dorothy L. Sayers, *The Man Born to Be King* (London: Victor Gollancz, 1943).

Whelpton, Eric, *The Making of a European* (London: Johnson Publications, 1974).

Williams, Charles, *The Figure of Beatrice: A Study in Dante* (London: Faber and Faber, 1943).

Yurdan, Marilyn, *The Oxford Book of Days* (Cheltenham: The History Press, 2013).

Notes

Chapter 1

[1] Letter from William Temple, Archbishop of Canterbury, to Dorothy L. Sayers, 4 September 1943, quoted in *From the Reformation to the Permissive Society: A Miscellany in Celebration of the 400th Anniversary of Lambeth Palace Library*, by Melanie Barber, Gabriel Sewell, Stephen Taylor (Martlesham, Ipswich: Boydell and Brewer, 2010), p. 577.

[2] When writing about Sayers as a child in her school days and before, I generally use "Dorothy". For a while as an infant she was known as "Dossie" – from her first attempt to say her own name. "Dorothy" means "God's gift", and her parents would most likely have been aware of the meaning when they named her. Her friends, including C.S. Lewis and Charles Williams, called her "Dorothy". Other friends called her "DLS".

[3] Letter from William Temple, *ibid*.

[4] Letter to DLS from Charles Williams, 13 August 1943, housed in The Wade Collection of letters of Charles Williams. Williams' point is rather similar to a challenge he made to his friend C.S. Lewis over his propensity to intellectually argue the case for Christianity, as in his book, *The Problem of Pain* (see Colin Duriez, *C.S. Lewis: A Biography of Friendship* [Oxford: Lion Books, 2013], p. 175). This reflects Williams' strong affinity with the influential Danish Christian philosopher, Søren Kierkegaard, who many regard as the father of existentialism and who perhaps helped to seed post-modernism.

[5] Her later review in 1955 of C.S. Lewis' memoir, *Surprised by Joy*, affirms the importance of the feeling of longing or sweet desire (*Sehnsucht*) in Lewis' road to God and then conversion to Christ, her response suggesting that her Christian belief did have emotional as well as intellectual depth (see DLS, "Christianity Regained", *Time and Tide*, 1 October 1955).

[6] She was eventually awarded an honorary doctorate in letters from the University of Durham. If she had accepted the Lambeth doctorate in theology, she would have been the first woman to receive one, a fact of which she was very much aware. There are many parallels between Sayers and C.S. Lewis, one of which is that he declined the honour of being made an OBE in December 1951 on the grounds that he did not wish to be associated in his beliefs with the Conservative government of the time, in his position as a well-known defender of Christianity.

[7] Acts 21:39.

[8] The memoir is *My Edwardian Childhood* and the novel *Cat o' Mary*. Her biographers, James Brabazon and also Barbara Reynolds (friend and Italian scholar), both demonstrate that the novel closely follows Dorothy's early life, changing the names of people and places that are easily identified. The memoirs are published together in *Dorothy L. Sayers: Child and Woman of Her Time, Volume Five (A Supplement to the Letters of Dorothy L. Sayers)*, (The Dorothy L. Sayers Society, Cambridge: Carole Green Publishing, 2002).

[9] Margaret Leigh, *The Fruit in the Seed* (London: Phoenix House, 1952). This would have been the famous "Alfred Jewel", referring to King Alfred the Great.

[10] The borough of Greenwich lies on the banks of the River Thames in London.

[11] The local name for the River Thames.

[12] I've not been able to ascertain which of the town centre streets accommodated the dentist's surgery. For an account of such memories see Sayers' unfinished memoir, *My Edwardian Childhood*, and incomplete novel, *Cat o' Mary* in Reynolds, *Supplement to the Letters*, vol. 5.

Chapter 2

[1] William Shakespeare, *As You Like It* (1623), Act 2, Scene 7.

[2] Associated with the sport of bandy, which was played on ice, here using frozen floodwater.

3 British History online, *A History of the County of Huntingdon: Volume 2*. Originally published by Victoria County History, London, 1932, pp. 153–58, http://www.british-history.ac.uk/vch/hunts/vol2/ (last viewed 17 April 2020).

4 Leigh, *The Fruit in the Seed*, pp. 32–33.

5 DLS, "The Fen Floods: Fiction and Fact", *The Spectator*, 2 April 1937, p. 611. http://archive.spectator.co.uk/article/2nd-april-1937/7/the-fen-floods-fiction-and-fact (last viewed 17 April 2020). Though after graduation at Somerville College Dorothy no longer lived permanently in the Fen country, but in Oxford, London, and other places, she is here locating her home as with her parents. When her father died in 1928 her mother automatically lost the tied house at Christchurch in the Fens, and came to live with Sayers in Witham, Essex.

6 Leigh, *The Fruit in the Seed*, p. 32. From Sayers' accounts and fictional portrayals of parsons, Henry comes over as more hardworking and conscientious than Margaret Leigh's thumbnail sketch of him.

7 Leigh, *The Fruit in the Seed*, p. 32.

8 Leigh, *The Fruit in the Seed*, p. 33.

9 Climate change is likely to dramatically alter the region as sea-levels rise. For the enormous impact of sea-level in the North Sea on East Anglia, see A.E. Trueman, *Geology and Scenery in England and Wales* (Harmondsworth, Middlesex: Penguin, revised edition, 1971), p. 143. Sayers points out the dangerous nature of the North Sea for the Fen country in DLS, "The Fen Floods: Fiction and Fact".

10 DLS, "The Fen Floods: Fiction and Fact".

11 DLS, "The Fen Floods: Fiction and Fact".

12 Leigh, *The Fruit in the Seed*, p. 33.

13 The classic children's story, Philippa Pearce's *Tom's Midnight Garden* (1958), is set near this area. The story tells how, in the particularly cold winter of 1895 (when Dorothy was two), Tom and his friend Hatty skated along frozen rivers to Ely on local skates called Fen runners (used in bandy matches).

14 Percival Leigh, *Comic Latin Grammar* (Fleet Street, London: Charles Tilt, 1840), p. 6.

[15] Leigh, *Comic Latin Grammar*, p.6.

[16] The medieval foundation of learning, where the three "roads" of grammar, rhetoric, and logic meet.

[17] See DLS, "The Lost Tools of Learning" in *The Poetry of Search and the Poetry of Statement* (London: Victor Gollancz, 1963), p.165.

[18] See *Cat o'Mary*, in Reynolds, *Supplement to the Letters*, vol. 5, pp. 65–66.

[19] *Cat o'Mary*, in Reynolds, *Supplement to the Letters*, vol. 5, p. 67.

[20] *Cat o'Mary*, in Reynolds, *Supplement to the Letters*, vol. 5, p. 67.

[21] See chapter 5.

[22] From *The Godolphin Book: 1726–1926*; see godolphin.org.

[23] See DLS, *Whose Body?* (1923), chapter 5.

[24] Katherine is Oxford-born and her pride in this was life-long, along with her father being head of the Choir School at Wolsey College for Christ Church in the novel.

[25] Miss White helped Dorothy in her studies for a scholarship by sending lessons in French literature by post.

[26] Oxford and Cambridge Joint Board Higher Certificate Examinations.

Chapter 3

[1] Vera Brittain, *The Women at Oxford: A Fragment of History* (New York: The Macmillan Company, 1960), p. 123. Brittain quotes from Vera Farnell: *A Somervillian Looks Back* (privately printed by the Oxford University Press, 1948).

[2] Brittain, *The Women at Oxford*, p. 123, quoting Vera Farnell's memoirs of Somerville College.

[3] Brittain, *The Women at Oxford*, p. 123.

[4] Legally, the courses at Somerville had been thoughtfully set up so that if the university in the future chose to confer degrees to women, graduates could receive them retrospectively, as Dorothy in fact did in 1920. There was however no assurance in 1912 that this change would happen, because of a deep-set cultural fear of women's emancipation.

[5] See https://www.some.ox.ac.uk/about-somerville/ history/ (last viewed 10 February 2020).

[6] Mary Somerville recollected: "Nothing has afforded me so convincing a proof of the unity of the Deity as these purely mental conceptions of numerical and mathematical science... the Differential Calculus... [and] the Higher Algebra, all of which must have existed in that sublimely omniscient Mind from eternity.... Age has not abated my zeal for the emancipation of my sex from the unreasonable prejudice too prevalent in Great Britain against a literary and scientific education for women.... The warmth with which [William] Somerville [her husband] entered into my success deeply affected me; for not one in ten thousand would have rejoiced at it as he did." (Quoted in "Luminary of Science: Mary Somerville" in *Somerville Magazine*, 2015, p. 17. http://www.some. ox.ac.uk/wp-content/uploads/2015/08/Somerville-Magazine-2015-pages.pdf (last viewed 10 February 2020).

[7] To explore this even in an introductory way would take a whole book in itself. There are a number of scholarly studies – monographs and books – of DLS's thought, in terms of gender study, feminism, insights into human creativity, the defining essence of the human being, the nature of work, social and cultural understanding, the impact of war, popular theology, medievalism, and Christian apologetics.

[8] See DLS, "The Lost Tools of Learning", in *The Poetry of Search and the Poetry of Statement*, p. 166; "amo, amas, amat" is from the conjugation of the verb "to love".

[9] Amphyllis Middlemore was only at Somerville for four terms before leaving for home-based accommodation for women in education under the Society of Home-Students in January 1914. The history of the Society of Home-Students is given at: https://www.british-history.ac.uk/vch/oxon/vol3/pp351-353 (last viewed 15 February 2020).

[10] For a connection between the MAS and the Somerville College novelists, see Susan J. Leonardi's extensive study, *Dangerous by Degrees: Women at Oxford and the Somerville College Novelists* (New Brunswick, New Jersey and London: Rutgers University Press, 1989), pp. 51 ff.

[11] According to Ralph E. Hone, quoting Charis Frankenburg, in *Dorothy L. Sayers: A Literary Biography*, p. 17.

[12] Hone, *Dorothy L. Sayers*, p. 144.

[13] Hone, *Dorothy L. Sayers*, p. 17.

[14] Barbara Reynolds, *Dorothy L. Sayers: Her Life and Soul* (Dorothy L. Sayers Society, Cambridge: Carole Green Publishing), p. 69.

[15] Account of the revelation to the *Daily Express* journalist given by Hone in *Dorothy L. Sayers: A Literary Biography*, pp. 32, 68–69.

[16] *Women and a Changing Civilisation*, p. 56; quoted in Leonardi, *Dangerous by Degrees*, pp. 57–58.

[17] See Leonardi's *Dangerous by Degrees*.

[18] Brittain, *Chronicle of Youth*, p. 213.

[19] See DLS, "Eros in Academe" in *Oxford Outlook*, I (June 1919), pp. 110–115.

[20] See chapter 5.

[21] See Leonardi's *Dangerous by Degrees*.

[22] The school is beautifully explored in Leonardi's *Dangerous by Degrees*. Other notable writers who were not novelists as such came out of Somerville, such as Sayers' cousin Margaret Leigh.

[23] Doreen Wallace's *The Tithe War*, was published 1934, a year before Sayers' *Gaudy Night*.

[24] A.L.P. Norrington, *Blackwell's 1879–1979: The History of a Family Firm* (Oxford: Blackwell, 1983), p. 63.

[25] Quoted by Hone, *Dorothy L. Sayers*, p. 25.

[26] Leonardi, *Dangerous by Degrees*, p. 57.

[27] DLS letter to her parents, 21 May 1913.

[28] Quoted in James Brabazon, *Dorothy L. Sayers: A Biography* (New York: Charles Scribner's Sons, 1981), p. 54.

[29] George Saintsbury, introduction in *Tristan in Brittany* (London: Ernest Benn, 1929), p. xxvii.

[30] See Barbara Reynolds, *The Passionate Intellect: Dorothy L. Sayers' Encounter with Dante* (Eugene, Oregon: Wipf and Stock Publishers, 2005), pp. 219–20.

[31] See C.S. Lewis, *The Allegory of Love* (1936) on Chaucer's *Troilus* in chapter 4, "Chaucer", and Spenser's *The Faerie Queene* in chapter 7, the latter depicting "the final struggle between the romance of marriage and the romance of adultery".

[32] Brittain had heard just that day of Victor Richardson's meningitis, from which he recovered. He was blinded in combat at Vimy Ridge in April 1917, dying from his wounds after two months. Vera Brittain's fiancé Roland Leighton died in action in December 1915, as did her brother Edward, June 1918. She tells their story in *Testament of Youth* (1933). A film of the same name, based on her book and diary, appeared in 2014.

[33] Brittain, *Chronicle of Youth*, p. 186.

[34] Brittain, *The Women at Oxford* (New York: The Macmillan Company, 1960), p. 123.

[35] It was later turned into Dorothy Sayers' novel of the same name, about the immediate aftermath of the marriage of Lord Peter and detective Harriet Vane, and much more. See chapter 8.

[36] Rachel Trickett, "David as Tutor" in Hannah Cranborne (ed.), *David Cecil: A Portrait by his Friends* (Wimborne, Dorset: The Dovecote Press, 1990), p. 79.

[37] See DLS, "Preface" to Chesterton's play, *The Surprise*, London, 1952, quoted in Alzina Stone Dale, *Maker and Craftsman: The Story of Dorothy L. Sayers* (Grand Rapids, Michigan: Wm B. Eerdmans, 1978), p. 37.

[38] DLS letters to her parents, 17–18 May 1914.

[39] DLS letters to her parents, 17–18 May 1914.

[40] Quoted in Brittain, *Chronicle of Youth*, p. 213.

[41] Leigh, *The Fruit in the Seed*, p. 59.

[42] More details about war-time nursing can be found in Vera Brittain's *Testament of Youth* and *Chronicle of Youth*.

[43] Brittain, *The Women at Oxford*, p. 123.

[44] David Coomes, *Dorothy L. Sayers: A Careless Rage for Life* (Oxford: Lion Publishing, 1992), p. 55.

[45] From a brief plot summary (student author unknown) quoted in Janet Hitchman, *Such a Strange Lady: A Biography of Dorothy L. Sayers (1893–1957)* (London: NEL Paperback, New English Library, 1976), p. 37.

[46] "The Bicycle Secretary's Song" includes the long "little list", snippets of which are here quoted. The song is only to be found in the typewritten script used by the student performers; it has never been published in full, to my knowledge. Stanzas from "The

Bicycle Secretary's Song" are quoted in Coomes, *A Careless Rage for Life*, pp. 55–56, and Janet Hitchman's *Such a Strange Lady: A Biography of Dorothy L. Sayers* (New York: Harper and Row), p. 22.

[47] Brittain, *Chronicle of Youth*, p. 263.

Chapter 4

[1] A.L.P. Norrington, *Blackwell's 1879–1979*, p. 63.

[2] As far back as January 1914, in a letter to her parents, she mentions a "ghost craze" sweeping Somerville, and that M.R. James' *Ghost Stories of an Antiquary* (1911) was in the College library, "very nice and nasty!"

[3] Outside the Classroom" in D.H.R by Member of Staff 1916–1935 B.H.S; 1935–1957 T.H. See https://www.flickr.com/photos/alwyn_ladell/18227747831/in/album-72157653224505489 (last viewed 18 February 2020).

[4] Charis Frankenburg wrote the autobiographical, *Not Old Madam*, *Vintage* (Lavenham, Suffolk: Galaxy Press, 1975).

[5] "Mr Geoffrey Pyke: Fearless Innovator", *The Times* obituary, 26 February 1948.

[6] The Godolphin School Old Girls [sic] News, Christmas 1915, https://godolphinww1.com/tag/salisbury-infirmary/ (last viewed 17 March 2017).

[7] See *The Encyclopedia of Science Fiction*, http://www.sf-encyclopedia.com/entry/jaeger_muriel (last viewed 18 February 2020).

[8] In DLS, *In the Teeth of the Evidence and Other Stories* (London: Victor Gollancz, 1939).

[9] A well-known example of this kind of poem is Tolkien's "Lay of Leithian" (concerning Beren and Lúthien). Never completed, the poem was published after Tolkein's death, in *The Lays of Beleriand* (1985), one of the volumes of "The History of Middle-earth". He began writing the poem during the First World War.

[10] See letter from J.R.R. Tolkien to Christopher Tolkien, 6 October 1944, in Humphrey Carpenter (ed.), *The Letters of J.R.R. Tolkien* (London: George Allen and Unwin, 1981), pp. 94–96.

[11] DLS letter to her parents, written in Hull around 30 January 1936 (exact day of writing is unknown).

[12] The letter was written to Muriel Jaeger.

[13] For more on the Inklings, see my *The Oxford Inklings: Lewis, Tolkien, and Their Circle* (Oxford: Lion Hudson, 2015).

[14] They met while Dorothy Sayers was working for Blackwell's, and Doreen Wallace a second-year student at Somerville.

[15] See Hitchman, *Such a Strange Lady*, p. 51.

[16] Hone, *Dorothy L. Sayers*, p. 31.

[17] Hone, *Dorothy L. Sayers*, pp. 31–32.

[18] Hone, *Dorothy L. Sayers*, p. 32.

[19] Hitchman's view is endorsed by DLS' biographer and close friend, Barbara Reynolds.

[20] In February 1919.

[21] Norrington, *Blackwell's 1879–1979*, p. 61

[22] Norrington, *Blackwell's 1879–1979*, p. 63. Basil Blackwell mistakenly remembered the length of Dorothy's employment. It was about two years, not three, with Dorothy leaving around June 1919.

[23] DLS had been greatly influenced in reading Chesterton's *Orthodoxy* while at school.

[24] G.K. Chesterton, *Orthodoxy*, chapter 6.

[25] My thanks to my friend the late David Porter, who brought the Maynard controversy to my attention while we were writing *The Inklings Handbook* together (2001). See also Reynolds, *Her Life and Soul*, pp. 81–82, and Grevel Lindop, *Charles Williams: The Third Inkling* (Oxford: Oxford University Press, 2015), pp. 73–75.

[26] Both reviews by Maynard were for G.K. Chesterton's *The New Witness*.

[27] Adapted from Colin Duriez and David Porter, *The Inklings Handbook*, pp 155–56. Used by permission.

[28] See Eric Whelpton, *The Making of a European* (London: Johnson Publications, 1974), p. 128.

[29] Whelpton, *The Making of a European*, pp. 141 ff.

[30] See Malcolm Graham, *Oxford in the Great War* (Barnsley, S. Yorks.: Pen & Sword Military, 2014), p.141.

[31] Vera Brittain describes the award ceremony of 14 October 1920 in her *The Women at Oxford*, p. 155–57.

[32] Mary Abbott, *Family Affairs: A History of the Family in Twentieth-Century England* (London: Routledge, 2003), p. 12.

Chapter 5

[1] W. Somerset Maugham, *The Summing Up* (London: Random House, Vintage, 2010), pp. 216–17.

[2] Sayers' letter to her parents, 2 November 1919.

[3] See her introduction in DLS (ed.), *Great Short Stories of Detection, Mystery, and Horror*, vol. 1 (London: Victor Gollancz, 1928).

[4] Letter to John Cournos, 27 October 1924

[5] Doreen Wallace is acknowledged by DLS' first biographer, Janet Hitchman, as a source of help in writing *Such a Strange Lady* (1975), to whom the book is dedicated.

[6] Quoted in Hitchman, *ibid.*, p. 54.

[7] DLS, *Gaudy Night*, opening of Chapter 1.

[8] There is no specific information on how Cournos and DLS met, but it is possible that 44, Mecklenburgh Square played some part in their coming into contact, and their restrained love affair. *Square Haunting* (2020) by Francesca Wade throws some new light on the cultural and social importance of the Square in that period.

[9] "Art and Ardor in World War One: Selected Letters from H.D. to John Cournos", Donna Krolik Hollenberg (ed.), *The Iowa Review*, vol. 16, Issue 3, Fall: H.D. Centennial Issue, 1986.

[10] The letters can be found in Barbara Reynolds (ed.), *The Letters of Dorothy L. Sayers 1899–1933; the Making of a Detective Novelist*, pp. 215–41.

[12] H.D. describes his room in her *Bid Me to Live*.

[12] Later, Lady Ottoline Morrell moved to London and continued hosting gatherings of members of the Bloomsbury Group. Cournos also met Yeats in Oxford city, in 1920; Yeats told him he liked his recent novel, *The Mask,* and invited Cournos to his house in Broad Street (John Cournos, *Autobiography*, p. 33). The following year Yeats invited a youthful C.S. Lewis to his house; Lewis vividly described the furnishings and odd ramblings of the wizard-like poet (Walter Hooper, ed., *C.S. Lewis: Collected Letters, Vol. I, Family Letters 1905–1931*; London: HarperCollins, 2000, pp. 530–32).

[13] John Cournos, *Hear, O Israel* (London: Methuen, 1938), Chapter XXV, p. 147.

[14] Sayers' letter to her parents, 18 January 1922.

[15] John Cournos, *Autobiography*, p. 332.

[16] After Cournos' death in 1966, his stepson Alfred Satterthwaite wrote a long, fair, and insightful article about his stepfather's life, "John Cournos and 'H.D.,'" in *Twentieth Century Literature*, vol. 22, No. 4 (December 1976), pp. 394–410.

[17] Possibly named after John Cournos.

[18] Sayers' letter to parents, 18 December 1922.

[19] The infant was first called John Anthony White, employing his father's surname, but later he was called John Anthony Fleming, sometime after Sayers married "Mac" Oswald Atherton Fleming in 1926.

[20] See *Cat o' Mary* in Reynolds, *Supplement to the Letters, vol. 5*, p. 140.

[21] His birth name was Arthur, but at some point he started to use "Atherton" instead.

[22] Atherton Fleming, *The Gourmet's Book of Food and Drink* (London: John Lane, 1933).

[23] Capt. Atherton Fleming, *How to See the Battlefields,* from chapter 3, "The Somme and Cambrai" (New York: Funk and Wagnalls Company, 1919), pp. 44–45.

[24] The pub was located at 67, Fleet Street, but closed down in 1971.

[25] Sayers' letter to Ivy Shrimpton, 15 March 1926.

[26] See Janet Hitchman, *Such a Strange Lady*.

Chapter 6

[1] In *Basil*, in *Complete Works of Wilkie Collins: Novels, Short Stories, Plays and Memoirs* (e-artnow, 2015; contact info@artnow.org; ISBN 978-80-268-3757-2; Apple Books), p. 5193.

[2] See Brian Sibley, *The Book of Guinness Advertising* (Enfield, Middlesex: Guinness Books, 1985).

[3] "Dorothy L. Sayers", in Ian Brunskill (ed.), *Great Lives: A Century in Obituaries* (London: Times Books, 2007), pp. 168–70.

[4] Quoted in theguardian.com, 11 June 2008: https://www.theguardian.com/books/2008/jun/11/dorothylsayers (last viewed 20 April 2020).

[5] Sayers' letter to her parents, 15 June 1922.

[6] I am indebted to Seona Ford for this observation, noted in The Dorothy L. Sayers Society Bulletin, Spring 2018.

[7] Campaigning began with Benson's on 28 September 1926, and ran until March 1933.

[8] Quoted in Brabazon's *Biography*, p. 135.

[9] The portrait and drawing are placed in the illustrations following p. 44 in Brabazon's *Biography*.

[10] Brabazon's *Biography*, p. 135.

[11] Sibley, *The Book of Guinness Advertising*, p. 88.

[12] Sayers' letter to her mother, 12 July 1926.

[13] In R.A. Bevan's obituary in *The Times,* 7 January 1975, R.D. Bloomfield, a former colleague, says: "Asked about the characters in this book [*Murder Must Advertise*] Bevan once said to me, 'Miss Meteyard was Dorothy herself.'"

[14] Janet Hitchman, *Such a Strange Lady*, p. 59.

[15] From "The Lost Tools of Learning", given as a lecture in 1947, and published as a pamphlet in 1948. Taken from Sayers' *The Poetry of Search and the Poetry of Statement*, p. 157.

[16]. James Brabazon, in his biography, writes that the house was known locally as Cocksparrow Hall, and that Ivy changed its name to The Sidelings. Today, however, there is a house called Cocksparrow Hall that stands as a neighbour to The Sidelings.

[17] Janet Gyford, "Mike Wadhams and 'Cocksmiths' (22–26 Newland Street. Witham)", in *Essex Archaeology and History News*, no. 111, April 1991.

Chapter 7

[1] Sayers pointed out that the book of Susanna was one of the first detection stories. See Dorothy L., Sayers (Ed.) Introduction to *Great Short Stories of Detection, Mystery, and Horror*, vol. 1 (London: Victor Gollancz, 1928), p. 9.

² Cleveland Moffett, *Through the Wall* (1909), accessed via *Project Gutenberg*, http://www.gutenberg.org/files/11373/11373-h/11373-h.htm (last viewed 21 December 2020).

³ She perhaps had Sayers in mind when she offered this advice in her preface to *Ask a Policeman* – or was she thinking of her Belgian detective, Poirot?

⁴ It was read out by Bishop Bell, with whom Sayers had become well acquainted in later years. The extract is from Lesley Walmsley (ed.), "A Panegyric for Dorothy L. Sayers" in *C.S. Lewis: Essay Collection and Other Short Pieces* (London: HarperCollins, 2000), pp. 567–70.

⁵ DLS, *Whose Body?* (1923), *Clouds of Witness* (1926), *Unnatural Death* (1927) [in USA, titled *The Dawson Pedigree* (1928)], *The Unpleasantness at the Bellona Club* (1928), *Lord Peter Views the Body* (1928), with *Strong Poison* (1930) in preparation, as well as a crime novel that did not feature Lord Peter, and which was co-authored with Robert Eustace: *The Documents in the Case* (1930).

⁶ Australian novelist, playwright, and historian, born 1897. After Simpson's untimely death in 1940, Sayers wrote a tribute to her in *The Fortnightly* (London: Chapman and Hall), vol. 155, January 1941, pp. 54–59.

⁷ Later he wrote as Francis Iles, as in his *Malice Aforethought* (1931).

⁸ In her preface to *Ask a Policeman*, in which six members of the club collectively created a mystery serial, Christie praises Anthony Berkeley as founder of the flourishing the "Detective [sic] Club".

⁹ G.K. Chesterton, "The Detection Club" in *Strand Magazine*, 1933, p. 462, quoted in "Seventy Years of Swearing Upon Eric the Skull: Genre and Gender in Selected Works by Detection Club Writers Dorothy L. Sayers and Agatha Christie" – a dissertation submitted to Kent State University in partial fulfilment of the requirements for the degree of Doctor of Philosophy by Monica L. Lott, May 2013.

¹⁰ She knew the talented Victor Gollancz well as an editor with her publisher Benn, who subsequently set up his own, highly successful, publishing house.

[11] DLS (ed.), *Great Short Stories of Detection, Mystery, and Horror*, vol. 1 (London: Victor Gollancz, 1928), pp. 9–10. A majority of the five tales concern his detective, Chevalier C. Auguste Dupin (the forerunner of sleuths such as Sherlock Holmes and Lord Peter Wimsey), and are: "The Murders in the Rue Morgue" (1841), "The Mystery of Marie Rogêt" (1842), "The Purloined Letter" (1844), "The Gold Bug" (1843) and "Thou Art the Man" (1844).

[12] From "The Vindictive Story of the Footsteps that Ran" in *Lord Peter Views the Body* (1928), broadcast 10 January 1939, at 7:30 p.m.; the play was written and produced by John Cheatle.

[13] P.D. James, *Talking About Detective Fiction* (Oxford and London: Bodleian Library and Faber and Faber, 2010), pp. 18–19.

[14] This brought together a large group of collaborators which included: G.K. Chesterton, Canon Victor L. Whitechurch, G.D.H. and M. Cole, Henry Wade, Agatha Christie, John Rhode, Milward Kennedy, Sayers, Ronald Knox, Freeman Wills Crofts, Edgar Jepson, Clemence Dane, and Anthony Berkeley.

[15] Quoted in Maisie Ward, *Gilbert Keith Chesterton* (London: Sheed & Ward, 1944), p. 468.

[16] Named *Suspicious Characters* in the US edition later that year.

[17] This could perhaps be a sign of encroaching dementia.

[18] See her cousin's visits to Bluntisham in Sayers' youth in chapter 2.

[19] See James Brabazon's *Biography*, p. 151. The biography was authorized by Sayers' son, Anthony Fleming, after his relationship with DLS had been publicly revealed, for the first time, seventeen years after her death, with the publication of Janet Hitchman's *Such a Strange Lady* in 1975. Sayers had wished that no biography of her would appear until fifty years after her death.

Chapter 8

[1] From Agatha Christie's preface in *Ask a Policeman* by members of the Detection Club, Eightieth Anniversary Edition (London: Harper, 2013), p. xv.

[2] See Sayers' letter to her publisher Victor Gollancz, 26 September 1935.

[3] Brittain, *The Women at Oxford*, p. 124.

[4] See chapter 3.

[5] Sayers' letter to Muriel St Clare Byrne, 14 February 1935.

[6] Sayers' letter to C.S. Lewis, date unknown.

[7] Agatha Christie's preface in *Ask a Policeman*. In Martin Edwards' foreword to the edition, he comments that Agatha Christie wrote her preface "in 1945, at the request of the Ministry of Information, for publication in a Russian magazine. Presumably because she was confident that none of her peers in the Detection Club would come across her comments, she was quite candid".

[8] In a letter to his son Christopher on 25 May 1944.

[9] Ann Loades, "Dorothy L. Sayers", in Lindsay Jones (ed.), *Encyclopedia of Religion* (Detroit, USA: Macmillan Reference, vol. 12, second edition, 2005), p. 8142.

[10] The play was published, and then included in *Famous Plays of 1937* (London: Victor Gollancz Ltd, 1937), pp. 285–428.

[11] Sayers' letter to Ivy Shrimpton, 21 August 1934. PTSD was common among survivors of conflict in the First World War. In her stories, Sayers has Lord Peter afflicted with likely symptoms of such stress.

[12] They apparently first met on the doorstep of a mutual London dentist's around October 1941 according to Sayers' letter to T.S. Eliot on 16 October 1941.

[13] London: Faber and Faber Limited, 1939.

[14] Ann Loades, "Dorothy L. Sayers", in Jones (ed.), *Encyclopedia of Religion*, p. 8142.

[15] C.S. Lewis, "A Panegyric For Dorothy L. Sayers", in Lesley Walmsley (ed.), *C.S. Lewis*, pp. 567–70.

[16] See chapter 4.

[17] From the cover jacket of the first edition of *Essays Presented to Charles Williams*, edited by C.S. Lewis (London: Oxford University Press, 1947). Sayers would be a leading contributor.

[18] Published January 1934.

[19] Quoted in Reynolds, *Her Life and Soul*, p. 242.

[20] Grevel Lindop, *Charles Williams*, pp. 97–98.

[21] Blamires was under Lewis' tutorage at Oxford, and the two became friends. See Colin Duriez, *J.R.R. Tolkien and C.S. Lewis: The Story of Their Friendship* (Stroud, Gloucestershire: Sutton Publishing, 2003), pp. 73–74.

[22] Quoted in translation by Sylvanius Urban, Gent., *The Gentleman's Magazine & Historical Chronicle,* Vol. 42 (London,1772), p. 261.

[23] Sayers' letter to Laurence Irving, 26 February 1937.

[24] R.C. Moberly, *Atonement and Personality* (London: Murray, 1901), p. 174.

[25] John Thurmer, *A Detection of the Trinity* (Exeter: The Paternoster Press,1984), p. 49.

[26] From, DLS, "Is There a Definite Evil Power?" in Ronald Selby Wright (ed.), *Asking Them Questions: A Selection* (London: Oxford University Press, 1953), pp. 49–52.

Chapter 9

[1] From Martin Edwards' foreword to *Ask a Policeman* (London: Harper, 2013, eightieth edition), p. xi.

[2] Lewis once commented in *Encounter* magazine that Sayers probably was unaware of the existence of the Inklings – an all-male circle of literary friends around Lewis. Charles Williams, a member of the group, however, wrote of a such a circle surrounding Lewis which met at Magdalen College. Sharing Sayers' humour and skill with literary allusion and play, Williams described Lewis in his correspondence with her as the King of Camelot. It was almost certainly clear to her that while Lewis was King of the Court, Williams would be Taliessin, the Welsh poet of Arthur's Court. Taliessin was a central figure in Williams' outstanding cycle of Arthurian poems. Williams told her that, at Magdalen, he had shared some of her delightful responses to reading Dante, found in her letters to him, with Camelot (letters which were to make up much of her essay in the posthumous tribute, *Essays Presented to Charles Williams*).

[3] Ann Loades, preface to *Dorothy L. Sayers: The Christ of the Creeds & Other Broadcast Messages to the British People during World War II* (Hurstpierpoint, West Sussex: The Dorothy L. Sayers Society, 2008), p. v.

[4] See Sayers' preface to *The Devil to Pay* (London: Victor Gollancz, 1930), p. 7.

[5] J.R.R. Tolkien, "On Fairy-Stories" in C.S. Lewis (ed.) *Essays Presented to Charles Williams*, p. 83.

[6] Richard Baxter, *Church-history of the Government of Bishops* (1680).

[7] Letter to DLS, 14 December 1945 in Walter Hooper (ed.), *C.S. Lewis: Collected Letters, Vol. II* (London: HarperCollins, 2004), p. 682.

[8] See Walter Hooper, *C.S. Lewis: A Companion and Guide* (London: Harper Collins, 1996), pp. 33–34.

[9] C.S. Lewis, *Miracles* (London: Geoffrey Bles, 1947).

[10] Sherwood E. Wirt, "An interview with C.S. Lewis", *Decision* magazine, September 1963.

[11] See Justin Phillips, *C.S. Lewis at the BBC: Messages of Hope in the Darkness of War* (London: HarperCollins, 2002), pp. 191–220; David Coomes, *Dorothy L. Sayers: A Careless Rage for Life*; James Welch's foreword in DLS, *The Man Born to Be King* (London: Victor Gollancz, 1943); Val Gielgud, "Production Note", in *The Man Born to Be King*, pp. 41–42, and "British Broadcasting in War Time," in *Theatre Arts* periodical (New York: December 1943), pp. 708–14.

[12] Phillips, *C.S. Lewis at the BBC*, p. 191.

[13] *The Times*, 27 December 1938.

[14] Phillips, *C.S. Lewis at the BBC*, p. 215.

[15] Val Gielgud, "British Broadcasting in War Time", in *Theatre Art* periodical, December 1943, p. 712.

[16] Around this time, J.B. Phillips, a friend of C.S. Lewis', was translating the New Testament into contemporary English – his objective, like Sayers with her radio drama, was to present Jesus Christ as he was: a real human being of his time, as well as divine.

[17] Sayers' letter to A.H. Ross, 19 December 1946.

[18] This is beautifully set out in a study by historian Mo Moulton in her group biography, *Mutual Admiration Society* (London: Corsair, 2019).

[19] James Brabazon, *Biography*, p. 184, where he states, "only two books actually appeared", not revealing the name of the second. The second was in fact *Masters of Reality*, written by Una Ellis-Fermor (London: Methuen, 1942).

[20] From Appendix: "Statement of Aims for the proposed *Bridgehead* [sic] series of books" in James Brabazon, *Biography*.

[21] Moulton, *Mutual Admiration Society*, p. 275.

[22] See Reynolds' chapter "Search or Statement?" in *The Passionate Intellect*.

[23] See Reynolds, *Her Life and Soul*, p. 402.

[24] See DLS, "…And Telling You a Story", p. 1., in *Essays Presented to Charles Williams*.

[25] Published by Ernest Benn, London, 1929.

[26] Reynolds' foreword in *The Divine Comedy: Paradise* (Dorothy L. Sayers and Barbara Reynolds, trans.) (Harmondsworth, Middlesex: Penguin Books, 1962), p. 10.

Epilogue

[1] From "A Panegyric for Dorothy L. Sayers" in C.S. Lewis, *On Stories and Other Essays on Literature* (New York: A Harvest Book, Harcourt, Inc., 1982), p. 95.

[2] Quoted by Mo Moulton in *Mutual Admiration Society*, from James Brabazon's biography of DLS.

[3] Alzina Stone Dale (ed.), *Dorothy L. Sayers: The Centenary Celebration* (New York: Walker and Company, 1993), p. 20.

[4] Hitchman, *Such a Strange Lady*.

Index

Adventurers All 74, 76
agnosticism 53, 59, 164
Ahasuerus 39
Aldington, Richard 91–93
Aldwinkle, Stella 171
Allen, Dr Hugh 61–62, 67–68, 92, 135
Anwoth Hotel, Dumfries and Galloway 129
archangel Michael 148, 150
Archbishop of Canterbury 17, 19, 85, 120, 168, 197
Ask a Policeman 127, 153, 169, 210, 213
Auden, W.H. 145, 157

Bach Choir, Oxford 61–62, 67, 78, 135
Bailey, H.C. 124
bandy 35, 199, 200
Barber, Marjorie "Bar" 90, 135, 146, 150, 168, 183
Baroness Orczy 124
Barton, Eustace Robert 124
BBC Children's Department 164, 165
      Children's Hour 163, 183
BBC Drama Department 166
BBC Radio broadcasting 10–11, 13, 17, 19, 41, 55–56, 110, 126–128, 151–52,
      157, 161–69, 184–186
Beatrice (in Dante) 61–63, 77, 158, 173, 175
      image of Beatrice 158, 173
      see also Charles Williams
Bell, George (Bishop) 144
Belloc, Hilaire 129
bell-ringing 23, 39, 139, 189, 190
Bendick, Catherine 58, 59
Benson's, S.H. (Advertising agency) 97, 104, 107–19, 123, 169, 182–84
Bentley, E.C. 124, 127, 184
Berkeley, Anthony 124, 127
Bevan, R.A. 112, 210
Biggs, Miss 76
Birmingham 140
Bishop Bell 145, 210
Blackwell, Basil 58, 70, 74, 76, 78, 80–82
Blackwell's 14, 74, 76, 78, 80–83, 87
Blamires, Harry 145, 146, 214

Bloomsbury Group 91, 94, 208
Bloomsbury, London 73, 91, 94, 170, 180
Bluntisham, Cambridgeshire 9, 29–48, 65, 73, 76, 117, 212
Bodleian Library 13, 69, 146
Bournemouth 68, 71, 75, 91, 97, 151
    Bournemouth High School 71
    Bournemouth Palace Court Theatre 68
Brabazon, James 13, 110, 116, 170, 177, 198, 210, 212
Bridgeheads series 162, 169, 170, 185, 186, 216
Brittain, Vera 50–51, 54, 56–57, 58, 61–62, 67, 69, 79–80, 134, 203–204
    Chronicle of Youth 56, 202, 204
    Testament of Youth 203
    Women at Oxford 50, 134, 201, 207
Byrne, Muriel St Clare 54–55, 63, 72, 78, 87, 90, 131–33, 136–39, 142, 146–
    47, 150, 168–69, 176–77

Canterbury Festival 144–47, 150–51,154, 155, 185
Cardinal Richelieu 42
Carroll, Lewis 25
Chase, Eleanor 90
Chesterton, G.K. 10, 11, 38, 53, 63–64, 81, 82, 99, 123, 127, 164, 204, 206
Christ Church Cathedral 178
Christ Church Choir School 21, 23, 25, 30
Christchurch, Cambridgeshire 78, 84, 117–18
    Christchurch rectory 103
Christian literary renaissance 145–46
Christian society and culture 141
Christie, Agatha 121–22, 124, 127, 134, 137–39, 182, 211, 213
Chubb, Margaret 54, 57, 71, 72
Cocksmiths 118
Cocksparrow Hall 210
Colchester Cathedral Festival 187
Cole, G.D.H. 74, 124
Cole, Margaret 124
Collins, Wilkie 107, 185
Colman's Mustard advertising 109
Comic Latin Grammar 36, 200
Cournos, John 92, 96, 99, 108, 182–83, 207–208
creation, human and divine 157–58
Crofts, Freeman Wills 124, 127
Cyrus the Persian 39

Dakers, Andrew 99
Dane, Clemence 127

Index

Dante Alighieri 4, 9–12, 38, 61, 63, 77, 154–58, 160, 162, 164, 166, 168, 170, 172–76, 186–88, 215
    see also *Divine Comedy (La Commedia)*
Death Bredon, Mr 113
Denver, Norfolk 33, 180
    Denver Sluice 33
Descent of the Dove 145
Detection Club 41, 55, 122–28, 154, 169, 170–71, 177, 183–84
Devil, devilry 93, 147–48, 152, 155–56, 172, 185
    division and destruction 152
Dignam, Joe 129
Divine Comedy (La Commedia) 9, 10, 12, 38, 154, 156, 157, 160, 162, 164, 166, 168, 170–72, 174, 176, 186
    Inferno 172–73, 186
    Purgatory 154–55, 157
    Paradise 154, 157, 174–75
Dorothy L. Sayers Centre, Witham 13
Dorothy L. Sayers Society 177, 188
"Dossie" 35, 197
Douglas, Mary 45–46, 49
Dowager Duchess of Denver 33
Downham Market, Norfolk 33
Duke of Bedford 33
"Dull Red" 43
Dumas, Alexander 41, 43, 174, 180
Dumfries and Galloway 129

Earith, Cambridgeshire 29–34, 180
École des Roches 84–86, 125, 182
educated women 59, 90–91
Edwards, Martin 154, 213
Ellis-Fermor, Una 170, 216
Ely, Cambridgeshire 29, 30, 33, 200
Eric the Skull 9, 79, 83, 84, 85, 89, 96, 118, 120, 122, 124, 126, 132, 181, 182
Eric Whelpton 79, 83– 85, 89, 96, 118, 125, 181–82
Essays Presented to Charles Williams 10, 158, 186–87, 213
eucatastrophe (good catastrophe) 151, 156–60, 164, 169, 172 , 156–59, 168
Euclid 40

Farnell, Vera 51, 74, 201
Faustus 147, 148, 154, 155, 156, 185
Fehmer, Fräulein 47, 50
Fen country 31–34, 45, 78, 104, 137, 180, 189, 199, 200
Fen Floods 178, 199–200

Fleming, John Anthony (son) 17, 20, 96, 97, 98, 100, 103–106, 114–19, 131–33, 146, 177, 178, 183–88, 208

Fleming, Oswald (also, Oswold) Atherton ("Mac") 16–17, 99, 100–106, 109, 111–19, 129–30, 131–33, 140, 146, 151, 170–71, 181, 183–87, 208–209

Floating Admiral 127, 128, 170, 184

Forster, E.M. 129

France 64–65, 71–77, 84, 120–21, 125, 182

Frankenburg, Charis, née Barnett 54, 56–58, 63, 71, 73, 87, 170, 202, 205

Freeman, R. Austin 124

Friends of Canterbury Cathedral 147

Fruit in the Seed, The 21, 31, 198, 199, 200

Galloway 111, 130, 184

Garsington Manor, Oxfordshire 94

Gatehouse of Fleet 129

Gerrard Street, London 124

Gervase 147
    Gervase's Latin historical record 147

Gielgud, Val 164-68, 184, 215

Gilbert, Michael 177

Gilroy, John 109, 110, 111

G.K.'s Weekly 100

Godfrey, Catherine 63, 72, 73

Godolphin School *see* Salisbury

Goethe 154, 156

Golden Age of detective fiction 9–10, 12, 38, 41, 120, 122, 124, 126, 132, 136, 142, 155, 172

Golden Age of the Detection Club 9, 120, 122, 124, 126, 132

Gollancz, Victor 125, 143, 211

Grandmother Sayers 25, 29, 31, 42

Great Yarmouth 75

Greene, Graham 145

Greenwich, London 198

Guinness advertising 9–10, 107, 108–12, 114, 116, 118

H.D. (Hilda Doolittle) 91–95, 207–208
    Bid Me to Live 93

Hadfield, Alice Mary 158

Hankin, Mr 113

Haunted Policeman 188

Hear, O Israel 94, 208

Heath Stubbs, John 158

Henderson, Elsie 64, 65

History of the County of Huntingdon 30, 199

Hitchman, Janet 13, 58–59, 79, 106, 113, 188

Hodgson, Leonard 85

Index

Holtby, Winifred 56, 58, 79, 80
How to See the Battlefields 101, 182, 209
Hull (Kingston-upon-Hull) 12, 75-76, 78, 80, 91, 181
Hutchinson, Arthur 43
Huxley, Aldous 56, 72, 74, 79
Huxley, Julian 129

Idea of a Christian Society and Other Writings 141
image of God 59, 148, 149, 152
images 77, 94, 149, 152, 172–75
Imagists 91–94
Inferno (Hell) 187
Ingleby, Mr 112, 113
Inklings, the 11–12, 78, 206, 214
Isle of Wight 21

Jaeger, Muriel "Jim" 54, 58, 72–73, 78, 83, 90, 92, 206
Jayne, Mr 113
"John Gombarov" 93
Judaism and Christianity 94–95
Jude the Obscure 23–24

Kennedy, Margaret 58
Kierkegaard, Søren 197
"King of Camelot" 214
Kingsway Hall, Kingsway, London 107, 112, 116, 182
Kirkcudbright 129
Knox, Ronald 124, 125, 184

Lammas, Katherine 48, 200
Lawrence, D.H. 91, 93
Lawrence, Frieda 91
Lawrence, Miss 64, 65
lay theology 11, 142, 152, 154–55
Leigh, Frederick 21
Leigh, Great Uncle Percival 36
Leigh, Henry 106
Leigh, Mabel, "Mab" (Aunt) 21, 25, 29–36, 117, 118, 119, 130, 183
Leigh, Margaret (cousin) 20–21, 31, 34, 61, 66, 106, 130, 198–99, 203
Leigh, Mrs Maud (Aunt) 20, 34, 36, 44, 106, 130, 150
Leigh, Uncle Percy 118
Leonardi, Susan J. 59, 202
Levsky, Ivan 93
Lewis, C.S. 10–12, 20, 25–26, 38, 55, 61, 77–78, 105, 120, 122, 141–46, 152, 155–64, 171, 173, 186, 197–98, 203, 208, 210, 213–14

Lewis, Joy Davidman 142
Lichfield Cathedral 172, 173, 186
Liddel, Alice 25, 27
Lisle Papers 72
Loades, Ann 139, 141, 156, 215
London 90–177 (*passim*)
 44 Mecklenburgh Square 91–93, 207
 24 Great James Street 92, 96, 103–106, 116, 119, 136
Lord of the Rings 77, 155, 159

"Mac" *see* Fleming, Oswald Atherton
MacDonald, George 77
Making of a European 79, 84
Malvern College, Worcestershire 105, 185
Man Who Was Thursday 123
Man with Six Senses 72
MAS (Mutual Admiration Society) 10, 54–58, 63, 67, 70, 135, 151, 169, 170, 202, 216
Masefield, John 145
McLaughlin, Father Patrick 171, 186
memorial service for Sayers 11, 141, 177
mere Christianity 11, 161
Meteyard, Miss 112–13, 210
Meyrick, Winifred 101
Michael, archangel 148–50
Middlemore, Amphyllis 54, 68, 72, 202
Milne, A.A. 124
Milton, John 173
Miranda Masters 93
Moberly, R.C. 149
Moffett, Cleveland 121
Molière 47, 75
Morison, Frank *see* Albert Ross
Morrell, Lady Ottoline 94, 208
Moulton, Mo 14, 170, 216
Murder in the Cathedral 144, 147

Napoleon of Notting Hill 123
Normandy 84–85, 182
Norrington, A.L.P. 203
Nott, Kathleen 187

Old Tom Tower 34
"On Fairy-Stories", J.R.R. Tolkien 158, 159, 160

Orthodoxy 11, 53, 63, 82, 123, 206
Oxford 8-208 (*passim*)
    Addison's Walk, Oxford 26
    Balliol College 20, 63, 74, 146, 147, 186, 187
    Bath Place, Oxford 79, 84
    Brewer Street, Oxford 21–23, 25, 178
    Christ Church, Oxford 21, 25, 30, 34, 6–62, 85, 178, 200
    Cowley, Oxford 98, 105, 115
    High Street, Oxford 26, 64, 66, 79
    Holywell, Oxford 34, 79
    Longwall Street, Oxford 78–79
    Magdalen College, Oxford 22, 26, 78, 180, 214–15
    Oriel College 66
    Somerville College 9–10, 20, 34, 50–62, 64–70, 72–74, 78–79, 87, 90–91,
        112, 123, 130–31, 135, 170, 180–81, 184, 199, 201–203
    Tom Tower, Oxford 21, 23, 78
Oxford Poetry 74, 76, 81
Oxford University 44, 80, 86–87, 107, 145, 171
Oxford University degree 80

Phillips, J.B. 216
Phillips, Justin 165, 167
"Pied Piping, or the Innocents Abroad" 67, 68
Poe, Edgar Allan 125
Pope, Mildred 60, 76
popular theology 10, 11, 38, 202
Pym's Advertising Agency 112, 113

Quick, Canon Oliver 210

Rallentando, Dr 68
Regius Professor of Divinity at Oxford 17, 85
Reid, Hilda 58
Reynolds, Barbara 10, 12, 25, 55, 99, 176, 187–88, 198, 206
Rhode, John 124
Rhyme Club 55, 78, 79
Ridler, Anne 157
Ridley, Maurice Roy 63, 83, 146
Rieu, E.V. 175
Robert Eustace 184
Romance of Tristan and Iseult 60, 61, 76
Ross, Albert 169
Rowe, Dorothy 54, 67, 69, 71–75, 91, 151
Rowling, J.K. 102

Saintsbury, George 60
Salisbury 29, 32, 34, 45–47, 179
    Salisbury Cathedral 179, 181
    Cathedral Close 46
    Godolphin School 45, 46, 48, 50, 51, 52, 54, 63, 72, 90, 181, 205
Sassoon, Siegfried 79
Satterthwaite, Alfred 208
Satterthwaite, Helen 96
Sayers, Gertrude (aunt) 25
Sayers, Helen (Nell) 21–22, 26–27, 30, 31, 34–36, 40, 42, 45, 103–104, 115,
    117–19, 180, 183, 184
Sayers, Henry 21, 27, 29, 31, 35, 39, 45, 78, 85, 103–104, 116–18, 180, 183,
    199
Sayers, Raymond   75
Scott-Giles, Mr and Mrs 150
Shackleton, Sir Ernest 47
Sheldonian Theatre, Oxford 63, 80, 87
Shrimpton, Amy (aunt) 42, 98, 106, 114, 115
Shrimpton, Ivy (cousin) 42–44, 98, 100, 103–106, 114–19, 130–33, 140,
    183–84, 209, 213
Simpson, Helen 123–24, 150, 169–70
Sitwell, Osbert 79
Sitwell, Sacheverel 79
Somerville College School of Novelists 56, 58, 202
Somerville, Mary 52, 201
Southbourne, Dorset 97, 98
St Anne's Church, Soho, London 171, 186
    St Anne's parish House 170
    see also St Anne's House
St Anne's House, a Centre of Cultural Studies, Soho, London 170, 177, 186
    St Anne's House first course given 171
    St Anne's House Advisory Council 186
St Cross Church, Oxford 20
St Silas the Martyr Church 145
St Thomas's Church, Regent Street 187
Stachey, Lytton 94
Stoop, Cora 57
Striding Folly 188
Such a Strange Lady 13, 188
Sunnyside Cottage, Witham 117, 118, 130, 135, 177, 178

T.S. Eliot 10, 11, 94, 141, 143- 147, 158, 172, 186, 213
Temple, William 15, 17, 120, 168, 197, 210
Ten Commandments of Detection 125
The Everlasting Man 164

the happy ending (*see also* eucatastrophe) 151, 156, 158, 159, 160, 172
The Hobbit 155
The Pilgrim's Regress 155
The Place of the Lion 145
The Scoop 127, 184
The Sidelings, Westcott Barton 132, 210
Theodore Maynard 83
Thomas Cranmer of Canterbury 144
Thompson, Sylvia 58
Three Musketeers 41–42, 45, 174, 180
Thrones, Dominations 141, 185
Thurmer, John 149, 150
Tolkien, J.R.R. 11–12, 26, 74–78, 137–39, 145, 154–59, 168–69, 205
Tours, France 64, 65
Tovey, Isobel 114–15, 132
Trickett, Rachel 63, 204

Uncommon Order of Initiation of New Members of the Detective Club 125
University Church of St Mary the Virgin, Oxford 26, 66

Vane, Harriet 20, 59, 92, 100, 122, 135, 137, 139, 154, 182, 204
Vermuyden, Cornelius 33
Verneuil-sur-Avre, France 84–85

Wade, Henry 124
Wallace, Doreen 56–59, 71, 79, 84, 91, 203
Waller, Lewis 43
Walsh, Jill Paton 141, 185
Welch, James 161–67, 172, 185
Westcott Barton, Oxfordshire 115, 132
Whelpton, Eric 79–86, 92
White, Bill 96–98, 102–103, 108, 177, 182–83
White, John Anthony (son) 208
    see also John Anthony Fleming
White, Mildred 50, 200
William of Sens 147, 148
Williams, Charles 10, 11, 18, 20, 83, 143–48, 158, 172–74, 186, 197, 214–15
    The Figure of Beatrice 158, 173
Wimsey family members 141
Wimsey, Lord Peter 20, 33, 46, 63, 83–86, 102, 113–14, 121–22, 127, 137–39,
    146, 150, 160, 187, 213
Wirt, Sherwood E. 163
Witham, Essex 13, 15, 117–19, 123, 129–30, 135, 171, 173, 177–78, 183, 188,
    199

Women at Oxford 50–51, 134–35, 201, 202
women priests, idea of 163
Woolf, Leonard and Virginia 72, 94

Xerxes 39

Yeats, W.B. 94
Yorke, Dorothy 92, 95, 96

Writings and translations
of Dorothy L. Sayers

"And Telling you a Story" 158
"Are Women Human?" 152
Begin Here 185
Busman's Honeymoon 63, 73, 139, 140–42, 144, 146, 147, 151, 170, 183
Cat o' Mary 38, 41–42, 48, 99, 198–99
Catholic Tales and Christian Songs 81–83, 143, 182
"Christianity Regained" 197–98
Cloud of Witnesses 106, 111–12, 183
Creed or Chaos? 187
Days of Christ's Coming 56
Devil to Pay 147, 150, 154, 171, 183
Documents in the Case (with Robert Eustace) 182
Emperor Constantine 187
"Eros in Academe" 203
Five Red Herrings 111, 129, 130, 184
Gaudy Night 20, 58, 59, 92, 134, 135, 138, 139, 184
Great Short Stories of Detection, Mystery, and Horror (with her introductions as
    Editor) 181, 194, 207, 211–12
Hangman's Holiday 184
Have His Carcase 100, 131, 182
He That Should Come 164, 166, 183
In the Teeth of the Evidence and Other Stories 183
Introductory Papers on Dante 186
Just Vengeance 172, 184, 185
Lord Peter Views the Body 183
"Lost Tools of Learning" 37, 54, 114, 200, 202
Love All 151, 185
Man Born to Be King 10, 17, 56, 156, 160–67, 171, 173, 183–84, 215
Mind of the Maker 10, 17, 38, 142, 148–50, 158, 162, 167, 169, 170, 183, 184
"Mocking of Christ" 83, 143, 144
Murder Must Advertize 73, 112–13, 184, 210
My Edwardian Childhood 37, 38, 41, 184, 198, 199
Nine Tailors 22, 32–33, 34, 39, 85, 139, 143–44, 178, 184, 187–88
Op. I 76, 181
"Papers Relating to the Family of Wimsey" 185
Paradise (Heaven) 155, 173, 174, 175, 176, 188
Poetry of Search and the Poetry of Statement 202
Song of Roland 76, 174, 186
Strong Poison 93, 100, 184
That He Should Come 56

Tristan in Brittany 171, 182, 194, 203,
Unnatural Death 138, 181
Unpleasantness at the Bellona Club 138, 181, 211
Unpopular Opinions 185
"The Wimsey Papers" 141
Whose Body? 55, 73, 88, 99, 102, 121, 137, 138, 180
Zeal of Thy House 144, 146, 148, 150, 153, 171, 183